"From arguably the best political cartoonist this nation has ever
pr⟨...⟩ecade
on⟨...⟩irectly
to⟨...⟩, what
ma⟨...⟩ype of
br⟨...⟩

"Every West Point cadet should be required to read Lieutenant
Dangerous, political cartoonist Jeff Danziger's powerful memoir
about his four years in the army, when honor, integrity, and purpose
were as illusory as American victory in Vietnam."

— **David Cay Johnston**, recipient of the Pulitzer Prize,
an IRE Medal, and the George Polk Award

"Not since Tobias Wolfs' *In Pharoah's Army* has there been such an
honest and self-aware war memoir to come out of the Vietnam
conflict. Jeff Danziger's *Lieutenant Dangerous* belongs on the shelf
next to Wolf, Tim O'Brien's *The Things They Carried*, and Karl
Marlantes' *Matterhorn*."

— **Tom Bodett**, author and radio anomaly

"'I am not a weeper, but I sat on the bus to Ft. Dix and wept.' So
begins Jeff Danziger's youthful journey to the center of America's
Vietnam maelstrom. A 24 year-old Vermonter with a pregnant wife at
home, Danziger experienced the full-on nightmare of the Army's
Vietnam catastrophe. He saw everything combat – death, hypocrisy,
moral degradation, and the fervid futility of the mightiest nation on
earth bested on the battlefield by men and women fighting in pajamas and loincloths. He saw everything, that is, except the nominal
purpose of the conflict. There is no evidence of a shared cause with
our South Vietnamese 'allies,' no evidence that American soldiers
knew or cared about the Communist Threat, and no evidence of the
proverbial quest for glory that theoretically animates military endeav-
ors. War, he writes, is 'in an awful way, interesting, if you can avoid
getting killed and don't mind loud noises.' Danziger's purpose is to
inform, but he and we wonder what the story of the 55,000 squan-
dered American lives has taught us. Then the jungle; now the desert.
Then B-52s; now Predator drones. The more America's ill-informed
interventions change, the more they stay the same."

— **Alex Beam**, author of *Broken Glass* and *Gracefully Insane*

LIEUTENANT DANGEROUS

A Vietnam War Memoir

JEFF DANZIGER

STEERFORTH PRESS
LEBANON, NEW HAMPSHIRE

For information about permission to reproduce
selections from this book, write to:
Steerforth Press L. L. C., 31 Hanover Street, Suite 1
Lebanon, New Hampshire 03766

Cataloging-in-Publication Data is available from the Library of Congress

Printed in the United States of America

ISBN 978-1-58642-273-8

1 3 5 7 9 10 8 6 4 2

For Jan

People go to fight wars because they don't
understand the seriousness of what they're doing.

— JOSEPH HELLER

The Vietnamese are among the bravest and most wonderful people on earth. I hope this writing shows the deepest respect and appreciation for their culture and their history. Despite much study and effort, throughout my war experience, I never gained much mastery of their musical language. And they never could pronounce my last name.

Dummerston, Vermont
August 2020

1

It has now been more than forty-five years since my tour in Vietnam in the army, a period of time in which I thought I would think about the war less and less. The opposite is true. These days I wonder how such a thing could have happened, not just to me but to the United States as a whole. I am reminded from time to time when I am talking with younger people, and I have to force myself to *not* talk about the war. I have to make an almost physical effort to mention the war only in passing and go on to other subjects. They, after all, have the present to think about.

But if they do bring it up first, that's a different story. And when they do, their interest is often motivated by their own personal security. For instance, if there's one thing young people interested in my Vietnam War experience want to know about first, it's the draft. What if the draft were reinstated? How did it work?

The rules of the draft back then were sneaky and open to local interpretation, not exercised the same or to the same effect everywhere in the country. In these days of gender equality, it seemed strange that only males were required to register at the age of eighteen. Even stranger that they could avoid being called up if they were in college. That immediately struck my listeners as terribly

unfair, which it was. Why should young people who were fortunate enough to be in college not have to share the burden of the war? Why should other young people lacking the intellect or the money for college be sent off to risk their lives fighting? Didn't this hint that the thinking at high government levels was that if a young man were thick enough to get drafted, he deserved less from life? He deserved to be an infantry grunt. If you were dumb and poor you were expendable. Even today, I find that hard to explain.

There were other unfair exceptions. If a man was married by a certain date, or had a child by a certain date, the draft boards had to excuse that man from service. That was the law. If you were drafted and you didn't show up, they came and arrested you. You could go to jail, and then be in the army anyway. It was not only unfair, it was weird. And it got weirder.

For example, there was the somewhat secret stipulation that your draft board could not be changed from the location where you registered at eighteen. The draft boards were made up of local people in local communities. How they were chosen remains a mystery. But they had a normal inclination to protect the young people they knew locally, and choose for service people they didn't know. They had to supply so many draftees a month from the lists of those who had registered in their communities. A friend in my basic training company, John Stephenson, was from Montana and had attended Dartmouth College. He was in Hanover, New Hampshire, when he turned eighteen. After graduation he moved back home to Montana. The Hanover draft board, probably reflecting the townie sensibility, drafted him, and called him back from Helena. He was angry, unhappy with Hanover and with the beggar-thy-neighbor attitude of the New Hampshire people he had come to dislike anyway. Of course, the draft board in Helena probably did the same thing, drafting men not from local families but from away. To John it seemed to be a perversion of the idea of everyone sharing a national burden equally. And it was.

What if you really didn't want to go? I had to think. What if? But no one wanted to go. I found it hard to explain that a huge percentage of American soldiers didn't want to be American soldiers.

My draft board was in Peekskill, New York, and they did the same thing to me as they had done to John Stephenson. I had moved to Vermont after college. The Peekskill people were just as eager to protect their local sons, and since I was no longer local, they put my name on the list. For a year I had a job in Vermont at a GE plant that made machine guns for fighter aircraft, and the job had a deferment. My exact job was to produce industrial films to illustrate the destructive power of miniguns.

Miniguns were Gatling-style guns used to strafe the Vietcong and North Vietnamese army troops. They were very effective. Fired down from small planes and helicopters, they supposedly protected US Army troops, or so I felt at the time. It did not occur to me that miniguns were very high-technology weaponry used against an enemy who had just rifles and no aircraft. I did not want it to occur to me.

The deferment ended. The arrival of a draft notice had a strange effect. My father had served in World War II during some hellish island fighting in the South Pacific. He counseled . . . well . . . nothing. If I wanted to go to Canada or Sweden, he offered financial help. In the mid-1960s the arguments for and against the war were at best inconclusive and at worst highly suspect. Young people who were against serving may have been legitimately against violence and war and in favor of peace for all humanity. Or they may have been against the idea of them individually and personally leaving their lives of American ease and privilege for hot, dangerous, and demeaning military duty. I could have gone to Canada because I had the family backing, but not everyone could do that.

I had been raised in middle-class comfort, and the trade-off was obedience. You didn't necessarily do what you were told, but you did what was expected. The most powerful influence on a young person was the conviction that there were well-thought-out rules and everyone followed them. Wise heads had concluded that America had to fight communism. The only way to stop communism was to fight against it, whereas in fact the cure for communism was plain. The real cure for communism was communism.

Second after that conviction was the widely accepted idea that the United States was guided to do the right thing given enough time and opportunity. God had something to do with this — we believed in right and wrong. Our version of ourselves was a combination of the World War II victory, the Marshall Plan, and Louis Armstrong.

I showed up as instructed for induction because, in addition to the foregoing reasons, I had always taken the path of least resistance. I was not a protestor, at least not personally. The easiest thing to do was to let myself be drafted and then look for a way to keep out of the actual fighting. The army was, after all, a very big place. Many drafted people served in Germany, which didn't sound too bad. Some never left the US. In addition, the war was the subject of fierce national political debate. The war might end. The number of US killed each week was down to about two hundred, depending on whom you believed. The acceptability of this number was explained by the general in charge, William Westmoreland, as being less than the number of Americans killed on the highways each week.

In retrospect I am amazed that I was so obedient. I knew that I didn't want to go, although I had no strong objection to other people going. I knew nothing about the army. I knew nothing about the history of Indochina. And I had no idea where or what Vietnam was. A survey of Americans revealed that a scant 6 percent of Americans could find Vietnam on the map, and most of those did so by accident.

I had to leave my job at General Electric, which paid fairly well, and adjust to ninety-five dollars a month as a private. My wife and I had expenses — mortgage payments, car payments, heat and light bills, and so on. I gave my new truck back to the bank. I did so despite a law left over from a previous war. The Soldiers' and Sailors' Civil Relief Act of 1940 said that debts were uncollectable under certain circumstances when a man was drafted. I could have told the bank they would get no further payments until I was discharged. But that meant a depreciating car on which the same debt would be owed. So the bank sent someone, and he drove the truck away. Whatever money I had already paid was forfeited. This gave me a sharper sense of the changes to come.

The worst part of the entire change was that I had to leave my wife, a gentle and understanding person, alone in our old house, on top of a hill in New England, a lovely place but something of a misery in winter. She worked as a teacher at a salary of less than four thousand a year. She determined that she would keep the job, mostly so we could make the mortgage and not lose the house. It helped me keep my sanity to know that I would be able to go back there and pick up life where it had been.

2

I left Vermont for Fort Dix on a wintry evening from the Hotel Barre, a handsome old brick building that had a fireplace we sat in front of until the bus showed up. Then it was time to go. I am not a weeper, but I sat on the bus to Boston and wept. I realized that I was going to a military something little more than a dreaded mystery, to fight in a questionable war in a country that I knew nothing about and cared nothing about, to be trained to shoot and kill people against whom I had absolutely no complaint.

A major revelation awaited me. More than a revelation — it was a surprise, even a shock. This was in 1968. About halfway through my eight weeks of basic training I realized that the army itself was a mess. The training was phenomenally stupid, left over from World War II and having nothing to do with conditions in Southeast Asia. It was this side of mad. It was in the winter in southern New Jersey. We marched in the snow and did exercises in the blistering wind. At one point we approached a mock Vietnamese village full of snow. We trained with old rifles, M14s, which included taking them apart and putting them back together blindfolded. M14s were not used in Vietnam. The training cadre did their approximation of stentorian drill sergeants they had seen in movies, but no one took them seriously. We ran in boots and wore back-packs and learned close-order drill. None of this had any use in the war. And we did KP, kitchen police.

I was on KP duty with a friend one day, and at the end of the morning's work we were sent back to the barracks to rest during the afternoon shift. The Fort Dix barracks were old, frame buildings, poorly insulated and heated by ancient coal furnaces and water boilers. The water heater burned all day heating a large tank of water for evening showers, the only real pleasure of the training day. My friend, whom I will call Demetri, was a large, very muscu-lar African American man who had hurt someone badly in a fight in his hometown and had been given the choice by a judge of jail or the army. He disliked the army as much as I did, but I guess he thought it was better than jail. Or at least he thought so at the time.

The barracks had separate rooms for cadre, and in our building there lived two cooks, skinny white kids who that day had stolen several boxes of frozen strawberries from the mess hall. When Demetri and I got back to the barracks we found that they were attempting to thaw the strawberries by letting the showers run on them, wasting the precious hot water. Demetri grabbed both of them and hauled them into the showers. He beat them one by

one, probably as badly as he had beaten whoever it was back home. Their noses bled profusely. The scene, which I remember clearly, was steam, blood, strawberries, and hot water. Demetri seemed to lack restraint. I had to interfere, which he grandly acknowledged later probably saved their lives.

Since the end of the Korean War no one had done much in the way of maintenance at Fort Dix. The Vietnam War showed up as a surprise. Some modernization was in progress, but the basic-training facilities were low on the priorities. It didn't matter very much since our esprit de corps was rock bottom to start. The army may have thought that crummy housing and a generally crappy environment could somehow make us tougher. This was not true. The dumpiness of the barracks and the mess halls and everything else only confirmed the suspicion that the army placed minimal value not only on our comfort but also on the effectiveness of our training. Standards of physical ability had been reduced for wartime, together with levels of marksmanship and first-aid training. The food we were served was poor quality.

I was dragged into the army with clear assumptions about military orderliness and strict discipline. I had seen movies about World War II in which orders were followed. This was most probably the case. But not in the 1968 army. That was the beginning of the problem.

We marched off in the mornings to the firing ranges with M14s left over from Korea. We blasted away with these cumbersome things, attempting to follow instructions bellowed from a tower. I got the idea that none of us really cared whether we got a high score. We were not, for the most part, killers, and it occurred to many that if we were recorded as lousy shots, we were probably less likely to be candidates for the infantry. Some time later I found out that this was true. Infantry commanders, a strange group within the commands, set high standards for the troops they wanted. Only a fool tried to improve his aim.

Shortly after Christmas a strain of influenza went through our barracks. At Fort Ord in California an epidemic of spinal meningitis in the training barracks got national attention. Fatalities from meningitis at Fort Ord were numerous and got lots of unwanted press. Fort Dix showed concern that influenza might be a parallel embarrassment. The tactics against influenza had a moronic character such as is only found in the army. To control the spread of sneeze-borne contagion, for instance, we were directed to sleep with canvas tents over ourselves at night. These tents were made with a part of bivouac shelters. We fell asleep to the sound of endless coughing. The medical effect was less than nothing. This silliness was the army's tendency to do something even if the something was useless and stupid.

If anyone was actually infected and had the flu they were sent to a special ward of the base hospital. The doctors there fell into two categories — young doctors who'd just graduated and owed the government some years in return for Pentagon financing, or old doctors who had made a career out of the army and were waiting for blessed retirement. The cure, and there was only one cure offered, was extreme hydration, using vast oceans of sugarless Kool-Aid, sweetened with the artificial sweetener sodium cyclamate, which was banned as carcinogenic by the FDA a few years later. We were directed to drink somewhere around two gallons of grape sugarless Kool-Aid a day, and the nurses, who had to wake us up every two hours, kept records. After a few days of this torture we would elect to return to training, half asleep, half drowned, and nauseous.

3

Toward the end of basic training, when my loathing for my situation and myself had ebbed only slightly, I faced transfer to advanced infantry training. An inner voice warned me against having anything to do with the infantry, not out of fear necessarily, but out of the self-realization that I was not a fighter, not an attacker of enemies, not likely to join readily in assaulting anything. Most probably this would be discovered in an infantry unit pretty quickly. Then I would have to either fake being aggressive or suffer the lonely life of an identified partial coward. There was a solution, or at least I thought so at the time.

It was possible to sign up for special schools and gain stature as a specialist in a non-infantry role. The signal corps specialized in communication; the military police maintained traffic flow; the quartermaster corps took care of supplies and housing. Any of these beat the hell out of ground-pounding jungle warfare. There were other specialties — artillery, helicopter maintenance, transportation, and even finance, which seemed extremely safe for some reason. And there were areas where your civilian training qualified you to not get shot at — the medical corps, the judge advocate, public affairs, and lastly, intelligence.

Wags say that *military intelligence* is a contradiction in terms, but it is in some ways the most important of the army's activities. For example, and this is serious, the people in military intelligence are supposed to be able to answer the question, "Where is everybody?" Not just the enemy, but our own people as well. Where were our units at any given time, and did *they* know where they were? In a war like Vietnam, without GPS or instant communication, small units of our boys tended to get lost. They were, after all, out there in triple-canopy jungle. For guidance they had maps, more or less accurate, originally produced by the French, and they had compasses. But from then on the technology of self-direction disappeared. If a general asked where's such and such a platoon patrolling, someone had to know. Or pretend they knew.

The role of pretending to know where everyone was fell to the military intelligence people, or the MI corps. Army units got lost in civilized, well-mapped Germany, so the potential for loss was multiplied in a place like Southeast Asia. This was true unless you were a native, and even then the native Vietnamese actually knew very little about their country beyond their immediate village. But the military intelligence people had another crucial role, one that is celebrated in many movies and in a good many books. They were supposed to know what the enemy was doing. They had to listen to what the enemy was planning. And here is where I came in, listening to the enemy's signals and conversations.

Sitting safely listening to the radio all day and making reports about enemy movements and secret stuff overheard seemed like a good, safe job. It was more dependent on the radio than on a gun, and it required that the surroundings be quiet. So therefore, it had to be done at a distance from artillery and explosives. There was only one problem, and I loved this problem. One had to be able to understand Vietnamese. I had been fairly adept at languages, at least Romance languages. And the language course in Vietnamese had another advantage. It was a year long. It would cost me another year in the army, but one sometimes tends to make decisions based on personal safety. At about that time, March 31, 1968, to be precise, Lyndon Johnson announced that he would not run for president again and that he would turn all his attention to securing peace. At the language school some of us theorized that we would never have to use our new language because the war would be over in a matter of months.

The language school was near San Francisco, on a base called the Presidio of Monterey, a beautiful place, or so I had been told. Except that it wasn't. It was actually on Biggs Field, Fort Bliss, near El Paso, Texas. El Paso may have a lot of valuable features, but it is not San Francisco.

The school itself was part of a joint set up by the army and the air force. Our quarters were at air force standards — in other words, an improvement. Curiously, the air force lives better, anywhere in the world, than the army, and good for them. There was a swimming pool, a crafts shop, an air-conditioned movie theater, a well-stocked PX, gyms, and tennis courts. The usual army drilling and nitpicking were dispensed with since we were supposed to be involved in intellectual attainment. Classes were six hours a day with a language lab for two hours every night.

I have mentioned that I could understand several Romance languages even if not fluent. I thought this would help. To get into the school I had to take a language aptitude test, something the government gave to potential students, not only in the armed forces but also in the consular service and the CIA. This test presented a fake language based on cartoon strips and captions that got progressively more complicated as the test went on. But if you were sharp, you began to dope out the grammar and vocabulary of this fake language. It was almost, but not quite, amusing. And if you were familiar with any Romance or Slavic languages you could catch on quickly.

Ah, but Vietnamese is not a Romance or Slavic language. It is in fact an uneven combination of Chinese vocabulary and a phonetic alphabet invented by the French while they were enslaving the locals during their incredibly cruel colonization of the country. Early in their colonization they introduced the truck-mounted guillotine. *Vive la France.* The most difficult aspect for normally thick Americans is that Vietnamese is tonal, like Chinese. A word spoken in one tone, up or down or with a lilt, will have a distinctly different meaning from the same word in another tone. The Vietnamese phonetic alphabet was devised by the French missionary Alexandre de Rhodes, may he fry in his own fat. To get the pronunciation right he added seven vowels and six tones, plus two *d*'s and a number of other oddities that had no counterparts in Romance languages. In addition, over the centuries three distinct accents had developed: one in North Vietnam, clipped and precise; one for the middle part of the country, not as clipped; and one for the South, slurred and

imprecise. In further addition, the Vietnamese them-selves thought it amusing to add their own personal accents and peculiarities to the conversation. They took what amusement they could from daily life, understand-able in a country in constant conflict for centuries.

I add all this language about language to back up the conclusion that for Americans who were smart enough to pass the test, meaning smarter than most but not much, learning Vietnamese was a slow process. But since the war was still going on, it was not all that unattractive. To learn enough of this melodic tongue to be able to figure out what intercepted enemy messages meant was difficult, close to impossible. In addition, the army had screwed this up as well. We were taught the southern dialect, somewhat lazy and singsong. There's the letter *d*, for example. There are two *d*'s. One has a little dash across the upright, and the other one doesn't, and it's called the soft *d*. In the South the soft *d* is pronounced as a *y* in English. In the middle part of Vietnam, it is pronounced as a *j* sort of sound. In the North it is pronounced as a hard *z* as in *zip*. I beg your indulgence.

By the end of the 1960s most of the enemy were North Vietnamese natives and spoke the northern dialect. Could we understand the northern dialect? Well, I couldn't. Examples of messages intercepted by the listening posts, and then transmitted by the technology of the day, were scratchy, inexact, and garbled. The language labs in the evening proved all that. We were given sample recordings from the field. About halfway through the course I realized that I could barely understand the gist of what was said in the radio transmissions, let alone accurate details.

If the army at any time questioned how effective their language instruction was, they did nothing about it. The contract for the school was held by a sloppy consortium of American language schools: Lacaze, Sanz, and Vox. They hired native Vietnamese-language teachers from France and Montreal who, evidently desperate for work, found themselves in the wastes of West Texas teaching groups of sullen enlisted men in prescribed rote lessons. The teachers were instructed by the contractors' management to stick strictly to the lesson schedule. The teaching method was endless repetition, and I suppose for some people, perhaps very young children, this method works. It didn't work for us. There are grammatical and syntactical rules in Vietnamese, but these were not to be revealed. Not intentionally anyway. If we figured out the strange system of classification characteristic of many Asian languages, we would be able to more easily, more quickly learn. But the method was repetition not understanding. The secret ingredient was time, and since the Lacaze, Sanz, and Vox contract paid by hours taught, there was no shortage of this secret ingredient.

There were other means of getting assigned to the language school, even more suspicious than the language aptitude exam. In my class there were several students with no aptitude at all. The army's assumption that the contractors could teach anyone was based on the contractors' solemn guarantee that they could teach even the least able soldier to understand an Asian language. One such example was an affable fellow named Sergeant Herman McKern. He outranked us all with some promotions he had received in a reserve unit back in his native Minnesota. His affability shielded him from a full understanding of the fun that was made of him as he tried to learn any vocabulary. But the truth was, he had no facility in this field. None. He stumbled through the daily repetition exercises, taking twice as long as anyone else, blissfully unaware of how painful the delay was for the rest of us and certainly for the instructor. One gets used to having time wasted in ridiculous ways in the army, but Herman McKern was something special. He also specialized in Yogi Berra–like sayings having to do with the history of the universe. He once opined that the earth was larger than the moon, but they were both about the same distance apart.

Minor rebellions were staged against the constant flow of idiocy. But the students were interested, as I was, in using up as much time as possible. We hoped the war would end without our direct participation. The result was dull acceptance of a moronic situation. There were two ameliorating factors. First was that about half the teachers were extremely pretty women, either Vietnamese or French Vietnamese. They wore the traditional garment, the *áo dài*, a pair of close-fitting silk pants under a long blouse, also close-fitting. The men wore, well, I don't remember what the goddamn men wore. But the women, girls actually, were a serious problem. They were graceful, dewy, with glistening black hair and lovely voices. I was very happily married and endlessly worried about my wife's security back home in our drafty old Vermont farmhouse. But if I hadn't been married, I would have suffered the desperate frustration of many of my fellow warriors. At the end of the yearlong course my roommate disappeared, AWOL, with one of the teachers and was never heard from again, at least not by me. Her name was Nga.

A second relief from the endless tedium of the school was a sharpening, almost a vicious honing of our sense of humor. Our targets were, of course, the upper ranks, officers and so on. In one part of the classroom building there were shorter courses, ten weeks or so, for officers and non-commissioned officers of the Green Berets. The Green Berets were an elite unit, or so they had been told. They were trained in tactics, medicine, civil affairs, and other things useful in winning hearts and minds. They needed to know enough language to get the confidence of the local population. But they were not any smarter than us devalued enlisted men. Of course, being elite they were more dedicated to the glorious mission of anti-communism in Southeast Asia. During the breaks we all mingled outside to smoke. My friend Steven Shackles was a partner in subtle insult creativity. Private Shackles devised a bit of theater in which we would pretend to be speaking very fast, very skillful Vietnamese. These were actually all nonsense noises that sort of sounded like the real thing. We did this purposely within earshot of the Green Berets. We would rattle off a bunch of utter blither that sounded like Vietnamese. Shackles would argue with me about some obscure point of grammar that he had just made up. And then to rub salt in the joke he would turn to a major, who was listening, lost and dumbfounded, and ask him a deadly serious question about the meaning of a word Shackles had just created. The extent of Shackles's creativity was boundless. The words he made up to confuse the baffled officer would be extra silly, something like *boo ba bah*. We then argued back and forth about the correct pronunciation or usage or tone of *boo ba bah*. Shackles had an incredibly valuable skill, at least in this context, of not laughing when things were beyond hysterical. I got better at this with practice.

The purpose of this silliness was to make the officers feel bad that we lesser enlisted mortals were so adept at Vietnamese, whereas they, who outranked us, were hopelessly behind. The problem with the whole act was that we were the only ones who got the joke. We were so desperate for amusement that we had to make up dimwitted pranks and play them on the easily victimized, all to absolutely no effect. Even so, I remember that at the time the effect of demoralizing those who outranked us seemed to be worthwhile. I don't know what happened to Shackles, but he must have had a future in something clever and funny and cruel.

But I would add in mitigation that neither Shackles nor I was abnormally mean. We were driven nuts in a subtle way by the situation, cooped up in West Texas with total strangers who didn't want to be there any more than we did, learning a goofy unnatural language, standing in lines every morning for attendance to be taken, having our heads shaved to military length, having our living quarters inspected for invisible dust, and, for most of us, having no social life. Plus being cooped up with Sergeant McKern. The more of this situation we accepted, the odder our thinking became. We thought of ways of torturing the officers because we felt justified. In a society with military ranks, you tend to blame people who outrank you as responsible for the way things are: the weather, the loneliness, and the war.

Shackles, for example, had no girlfriend or wife, and the celibacy was driving him crazy in another way. I remember him as tall and good-looking. He gawked at the local girls when we went to the movies or the ball games, but he had no money to take anyone out on a date. I didn't want local dates, and my money was sent home to help my wife pay the bills. What happened to Shackles's money I don't know, but he was suffering. The worst effect came from the young Vietnamese women who taught us. They were the subjects of countless dreams. We were warned to treat them with utmost respect, but that was nigh impossible. In the novel *Catch-22* the men begin groaning every time a woman walks by. My fellow students would pretend to go into paralytic shock if one of the teachers showed up in particularly fetching clothes. The teacher would ask a student to repeat some sentence in Vietnamese, and he would comically collapse, his arms limp and his eyes closed, his mouth lolling open. It was certainly amusing. God knows what the poor teachers thought was going on. Shackles also indulged in idiotic acts of how much he was smitten by one of the teachers. He would stare at the teacher and stick out his tongue and make noises. He would snap his fingers and say, "That's what I'm fightin' for!" He made up alliterative descriptions of his devotion. I shamefully remember two examples — "I would eat the peanuts out of her turds." And "I would low-crawl across broken glass to hear her fart over a field phone."

The Vietnamese teachers were an odd group. Many were French Vietnamese and from middle-class families but now forced to work. Some were transplants to Quebec and for all intents and purposes nearly stateless. The US State Department wanted them here, but when and if the war ended they would have to find new homes. We were together for a long time and got to know one another fairly well. Ong Dien was one teacher, French Vietnamese, who realized that to keep his students awake he had to be interesting and animated. This also kept him awake because he enjoyed an active social life, not an easy accomplishment for an Asian in El Paso. El Paso was, however, a border town, and the population was mixed. Anyone Asian was Japanese in the simplified Texas view of the world. Ong Dien had dates, not just with the other Vietnamese teachers but with a variety of locals. He may have been bisexual. At the time I had no way of judging. But he was also an excellent cook. He made French specialties and was a wine expert. He had us to his house, a little southwestern bungalow with a roaring swamp cooler on the roof, for dinners. He ran cooking lessons on entry-level Vietnamese cuisine, spring rolls and pho. He also liked to drink, something I learned later was a strong Vietnamese trait. His fellow teachers gathered and got blotto, taking advantage of the cheap prices for tequila and scotch. The favorite was Johnnie Walker, which led to questions about who was this genius, Johnnie Walker, what did the name mean, was there actually such a person? I provided the translation — *Ong Johnnie Di Bo*, literally, Mr. Johnnie Goes By Foot.

4

Fort Bliss and El Paso are on the Texas–Mexico border. We had Saturday afternoons and all day Sundays off from the language training, and since we had very little money, Mexico had great appeal. Ciudad Juarez back then was not the drug-related bloodbath it has become today. It was a lazy entrepôt where one could get a steak dinner and lots of beer for three or four dollars. I had resolved meatlessness and alcohol abstinence while in the service on the wise advice of my father. Mess hall food was greasy and questionable, and his advice was good. I drank no alcohol. (For the record, I have made up for my military abstinence in the years since.)

The border economy had other attractions from which I also abstained. But I went with friends to Juarez, and in particular with a friend named Larry Fitchhorn. A bar and brothel named the Navy Rose had a social program for lonely GIs, and Larry fell desperately in love with one of the staff. An evening with . . . well, I don't remember her name . . . was ten dollars. The price was reducible if she felt some attraction beyond strict business. Fitchhorn was no Adonis, in fact he was a rather tough-looking specimen from Michigan's Upper Peninsula. But the girl had a calming effect on him, even though he was tortured by ideas of how to get her out of her current career. She was

pretty and spoke enough English to understand what he wanted, and how it might benefit her. What drove him substantially crazier was that during the week, when he was supposed to be learning a language that had no value and no meaning, and that might actually get him killed, the girl was still trying to earn money in her job. This made it difficult for him to concentrate.

At one point he wanted to borrow money from me so he could marry her and send her back to Michigan to live with his family until the war was over. He calculated that a sum of around two hundred dollars would do it. He had a detailed plan. They would get married in Juarez. She would go to Michigan by Greyhound. She had no money to contribute because, as she assured him, all her earnings went back to her tiny village in the mountains to help her poor mother and siblings. Larry was moved by this story, and I was, too, sort of. Just not two hundred dollars' worth. I am a little foggy on this, but I think I contributed $50, a considerable expression of my faith in the human heart since I was making barely $140 a month as a Specialist Four, and my own wife needed the money.

But Larry was grateful and assured me that he would pay me back, and he promised to name their firstborn son after me, and so on.

I am ashamed to say that I can't remember the end of the Larry Fitchhorn story, and I apologize for having gone on this long only to have nothing more. Love may have conquered all, or maybe not. I stopped going to Mexico and began a strict regime of running and biking and reading. I bought a bicycle and took long rides all by myself, planning my routes so that the West Texas wind was always behind me. I became a lonely authority on the subject. The wind changed throughout the day. In the morning it was easterly, and the opposite in the evening. Wind is the main weather factor in West Texas, howling day after day. Why people live in West Texas is a mystery to me, as it is to most Texans.

In addition to biking and running I began a self-directed program of reading. I read all of Thomas Hardy, all of Arthur Conan Doyle, the entire King James version of the Bible, and all, or nearly all, of Shakespeare. I read *The Good Soldier*, and *Catch-22*, and *The Leopard*. I even read the dictionary and made cards for words I didn't know. I grew more solitary and was of less and less interest to my friends. Supposedly you make close friends in the army, but it's not so, not even in the actual war part. The army, as William Manchester said, is like an empty room. People come in and go out, some having no idea why they're there and simply wanting to leave and forget. Most of my fellow soldiers were draftees — that is, they were in this metaphorical room under duress — and our interest in one another was never very strong.

If you have studied the period in American history, or lived through it, you will remember that outside the military the country was tearing itself apart. Riots roiled political conventions; National Guard troops fired on students. Vietnam was the most visible point of contention, and the older American national diseases — race, inequality, religion, sectional hatreds, and generational suspicions — were gaining strength beneath the surface. Strangely, inside the army the mood was characterized by resentful acceptance and nearly palpable disobedience.

Most of these effects were increased in the actual war zone when it became gruesomely evident how the benefits and costs were distributed. Stateside, the fault lines were made flagrantly visible by the press, some accurately, others blown out of all proportion. I became aware that, in general, I disliked everyone who outranked me, and felt pity for everyone I outranked, which was almost no one. Men of my own rank I didn't care about, and in a military sense, I had little interest in myself.

The enlisted men hated the commissioned officers, the draftees hated the enlistees, the junior officers hated majors and above, the lifers hated the civilian contractors. The army hated the air force as flyboys and pansies; the air force hated the army right back as slobs and killers; the infantry hated the rear-echelon motherfuckers; soldiers from rural America hated smart-asses from New York and LA. The smart-asses hated themselves for being lumped in with goobers and droolers. Draftees hated those who escaped the draft; escapees hated anyone who reminded them of their cowardly good luck. And of course blacks and whites, even those who could get along in civilian life, hated each other. I suppose some Protestants hated some Catholics, and somebody had to hate the Jews.

In general, everyone in the army hated the army, and thus by the end of the 1960s and into the 1970s the army came slowly to realize that the real damage was being done not to the enemy, but to the army itself, by itself. Discipline not only went to hell but in some units disappeared. Promotions, especially to command positions, carried such personal danger that they were not sought after as they should have been. A sort of command avoidance occurred so that the best commanders did not always rise in rank. Some didn't want to. It became apparent that the age-old guiding principle of all military effort was not only distant — it was probably impossible. This principle was, and is — and I guess should be — victory.

Typically, the generals can read the overall success or failure of the army's efforts and determine its chances for ultimate victory sooner than the lower ranks. But Vietnam was an upside-down situation. The generals lied, not only to the country and to the president, but to themselves as well. Division commanders and brigade commanders continued to seek the enemy, continued to plan huge operations with troops and helicopters and artillery and bombing missions. Men were shot, wounded, lost, driven crazy, and had their lives ruined, as in every war, but the goal grew indistinct and farther distant. Good morale, where there was any, was not lauded; it was suspect.

Meanwhile, my own plan to hide out in the language school until the war was over was failing, along with so many other plans. Waiting until everyone else came to the conclusion that there wasn't going to be a victory was not working. The language course came to an end. I was scheduled for another short course in how to work a radio and then deployment to Vietnam. In quiet desperation, I decided to apply to be an officer. I knew I didn't particularly want to be an officer, and that I would probably be a very bad officer, but officer candidate school was six months long. Commissioning supposedly also meant an additional stateside assignment of an additional six months. Surely, I thought, the damn thing would be over by then.

My younger brother, who left college early for reasons unclear, had become an infantry officer, and I thought that since I had already finished college, I would be accepted. My company commander at the language school did some research and told me that unfortunately I would not be accepted. My language training was considered too valuable not to be used in the war. Officer training could wait until I had completed a language utilization tour. This was bad news. All that remained was the six-week course in how to run a radio, and then off to the war zone. But there might be an exception. I could apply for a *direct* commission, no OCS, no running around and learning leadership skills. There was an outside chance that they would simply bump me up to being a lieutenant. Of course any stall in the inevitable was welcome. I filled out the paperwork, got pictures of myself standing at attention, and underwent a security check. I turned in the application and waited. Nothing happened.

During this time I had developed an unusual, or maybe understandable, interest in salvation, or at least I thought about it. Was there some sort of salvation? Could I be saved, maybe from being shot at. This was partly due to fear of violence in Vietnam, and partly due to the search for any comfort gained by thinking that good fortune favored good people. It was, as it usually is, more hope than conviction. My mother had an Irish sense that reading the Bible kept children, especially boys, from bad behavior, or at least made them worry while doing bad things. What I did enjoy, and still enjoy, was the language of the King James Version, the *thees* and the *thous* and the *doths* and the minatory admonitions and graceful proverbs.

I, along with most of my language class, and Fitchhorn by the way, was sent to study radio intercept at an air force base near San Angelo, Texas, a town smaller than El Paso, and lonelier and dustier. Then orders came, just as the course began, that I'd been approved for a direct commission.

This was good news. My pay would be increased. The only remaining hurdle was a board interview by a panel of three officers to test my moral worth and intelligence. I was taken off the roster for the radio class, although it was the first thing in my army career that I had looked forward to. The board was convened, and I showed up, starched to a fare-thee-well, shoes polished and brass gleaming. For someone who hated the army as much as I did, this act was nothing if not high theater. The head of the board was a colonel, flanked by two lesser humans, a major and a captain. I planned to answer the questions as I imagined a highly spirited young officer would. But as the interview came to a close, the colonel wanted to know what I would do if it became necessary to get some information out of a prisoner of war. Since I probably would be given a military intelligence role, I might have to face the question of torturing or otherwise encouraging an enemy to give up useful secrets.

The fact was that virtually no valuable information was ever gained from prisoners in the Vietnam War. The lines of combat were so diffuse, hidden here and there in the dense forests, that not only did the Americans not know where the Vietcong and North Vietnamese were, but in many instances neither did they. I answered the question with some convincing blather, and later I reflected about how good I'd become at blather. In no other organization than the army is it so necessary to be able to sound like you know what you're talking about. This is valuable training, and it has served me well since.

But the colonel turned out to be a Baptist or something, and a thoughtful man. Obviously, he detected that I was better with words than actual thought, and he pursued my inner convictions. He asked if I prayed and if so how. This was a telling question, and you have to realize that I was still fairly young, or in other words I had no convictions worthy of the term. But rather quickly I was saved by memory. I said I followed the advice "When thou prayest, enter into thy closet, and when thou hast shut thy door, pray to thy Father which is in secret; and thy Father which seeth in secret shall reward thee openly."

There was a moment of silence. Well, if it was good enough for Jesus it should be good enough for the colonel. And it was, although looking back, I see that I actually dodged the question.

Orders to make me an instant lieutenant were coming, and in the meantime there was nothing for me to do. My wife had joined me in San Angelo, about seven months' pregnant. We got an apartment in town and attended some of the San Angelo cultural events. Traveling orchestras were a big feature at the opera house, and the audiences were polite and appreciative. Each concert began with a trooping of the colors and the singing of the national anthem. I suspected Texas patriotism as being more for show and out of habit than from a genuine conviction. Sometimes the audience broke into some sort of Texas song, and once we all sang "Vaya con Dios." The young soldiers or Boy Scouts carrying the flag exuded youthful military enthusiasm.

I waited for more orders. So to eat up the time I was assigned as an orderly since I was still an enlisted man, making coffee and buffing the hell out of the floor, twenty-four hours on duty and forty-eight hours off. My wife had to go home to Vermont, in part because the airlines refused to carry women near childbirth, and partly because, for some dopey reason, we didn't want our child born in Texas. I didn't dislike Texas, but I found the large, loud, boastful people annoying and insincere. After my wife went back home I was left with two-day periods with nothing to do. There wasn't a lot to amuse me in San Angelo. There were go-cart tracks and miniature golf and a bowling alley, but I had very little spendable money. A man at the local church suggested that I might like to do some part-time work, helping tend the huge herds of sheep and angora goats he owned that roamed unsupervised in the endless miles of prairie outside the town. The owner lived in town, but he arranged for me to help his foreman, doing fence repairs and maintaining the windmills that pumped water for the herds.

Like a lot of Texas, the lands around San Angelo were windy, flat, treeless expanses. When it rained the grasses sprang up, and the sheep and goats had good fodder. During the dry spells they waited for rain. They were watered at large tanks that were steadily filled by windmill-driven pumps. The wind was constant and the windmills pumped steadily, gushing water into the tanks. When the tanks were filled, the excess water ran back down into the well. My job was to climb the towers and check on the machinery, replace any windmill blades that were ready to fail, and fill the little gearboxes with oil. The windmills went around, raising and lowering the column of pipes that went down into the well. The machinery was mildly fascinating. The sections of pipe were joined by clever couplings that contained a sort of flapper valve. The water was raised to the top sections, where it overflowed into the tank. I found this pretty amazing since the entire thing ran on wind, for free, without ceasing. The sheep and goats took it all in stride.

The foreman was happy to show me how to replace the windmill blades. He pronounced me a fast learner. I

think his name was Ron, but maybe not. He was about sixty, wiry and bowlegged. He lived in an extremely small trailer with two or three guns. He cooked for me and the other herdsmen on the back of a genuine chuck wagon pickup truck. Ron rarely went into town, due to his suspicion of city cupidity and sloth. He gave me a few disquisitions on what was right and wrong with America, which were not as verbose as his solitary life would have justified. Most of the other herdsmen were Mexicans and had limited English. I was a fresh set of ears. He liked the life he was leading and seemed very healthy. He admitted that this life wasn't for everyone, and he was pleased if other people would stay in their cities. He had been out in the Texas sun and wind for a long time, maybe most of his life. The skin of his face and neck were not only dark brown but also had the texture and sheen of fine shoe leather. His eyes were the palest blue and his teeth glowed white. Most impressive was his skill in rolling a cigarette with one hand. This takes a lot of dedicated practice, producing many failures and a lot of spilled tobacco. I hadn't smoked for years, but I started again because of the challenge.

I only worked for Ron for about five weeks, and then my orders came through. I told Ron that I would be leaving and that I had enjoyed working with him and would always remember my windmill experience. I said I had more training ahead, and maybe shipment to the war. Ron said that I should be careful — he had been in the navy and hated it. He said that he hated officers and that I should never trust an officer under any conditions. Okay. On my last day he said that when I had finished my duty, if I needed a job, I should come back down to San Angelo and look him up. If he had an opening, I was sure of employment. I tried to give him my car, but he didn't want it. None of the Mexican guys wanted it, either.

I had only a day or two to prepare to leave. My car had to be disposed of somehow. I quickly sold it to a fellow soldier for twenty-five dollars — fifteen down and the remaining ten to be sent if it was still running after one month. It was a nineteen fifty-something DeSoto, and it leaked every known fluid, including but not limited to brake fluid, steering fluid, oil, antifreeze, wiper fluid, and several other liquids known only to the Chrysler Corporation. In the trunk were potions that promised to free sticky lifters, prevent gas tank corrosion, improve mileage, seal radiator leaks, and stop valve clatter. The ten dollars never showed up.

So that was almost fifteen months in Texas, expended for the sole purpose of avoiding getting shot at in a war no one wanted or understood. It took me awhile to get over my distaste for Texas, and it may not be gone yet. My conclusion was that Texans, and American southerners in general, have a more ready acceptance of military solutions than do northerners. This is probably not completely true, but it seemed that way. Of the people I met in the army, stateside and overseas, southerners seem more attracted to going to other people's countries and shooting at them. Southern officers and senior NCOs accepted the role of beating the hell out of people who couldn't really defend themselves. There was a strain of bullying and pushing people around if you could, and a reluctance to think of others as deserving of equal status. God was involved somehow, with the explanation that if God wanted a fair deal for people in the benighted countries of the world, He should have given them a better break than He provided for us in the United States. Some Texans I met disliked equality in their fellows.

But not all Texans. In El Paso, I befriended a family of extraordinarily gentle and accommodating people who welcomed me and other soldiers for wonderful dinners out at their ranch in the Pima cotton fields. The head of the family agreed that there was a hidden strain of superiority just under the surface in Texans, not in everyone to be sure, but enough to make it worth watching out for. This is a human trait, but it's stronger in the individual when it's held by a large quotient of the group. In addition, there was a curious type of lawlessness as well, maybe left over from the frontier days, but still alive in finance and jurisprudence. Illegality, in the Texas culture, was simply what you got caught at. If you didn't get caught, then it was legal. The law was being constantly tested to see where it applied and what it meant. Texas was wild, less comfortable with itself despite its boasting. It seemed resolved to meet the world as a fight.

But I was a soldier fighting to defend Texans and their government. Even though I was forced to do so, I still tried to find something redeemable in the mission. Whatever it was it wouldn't be the weather. The extremes of wind and dust and heat and hail made me wonder if there was any real reason to live there. I suppose anywhere you are forced to live and forced to do work in which you have no interest, for a long period of time, in the company of others who are similarly cursed, can be at best unattractive. So as soon as my orders came through, I was happy to get the hell out.

5

I had assumed that if I got to Vietnam as an intelligence officer with the ability to speak and write Vietnamese, I would be assigned some peaceful work at the army head-quarters in Saigon, a city still reflecting the Indochinese culture, the residual French colonial influence, the colorful and attractive Vietnamese civilians, women in *áo dàis* floating by on bicycles, favoring me with a smile. I thought that the language and the rank would afford me far more interesting jobs than I would have had in the infantry. I had smoothly escaped its vile operations. I would be able to write intelligence reports in English and Vietnamese, something authoritative about this odd and sad war. Perhaps I would compose explanations, maybe a finely cloaked novel, a study of the interplay of politics and emotions that . . . well, you get the idea. That all seemed to make sense.

But it didn't. I was assigned to nothing having to do with military intelligence. In a blindingly unexplainable move, I was sent to train as an ordnance officer at Aberdeen Proving Ground in Maryland. I never learned why this misassignment happened or who did it. My first task was to find out what ordnance was. *Ordnance* means all the machinery of war, all the explosive stuff, artillery pieces, tanks, small arms, anti-aircraft guns, trucks and radios, mines and radars. Most ordnance management in an ordinary war takes place slightly in back of the front line, but in Vietnam, where there were no front lines, the mission was as awful as being in the infantry, and in some ways worse. My main task would be changing artillery tubes, arriving by helicopter and working on firebases in full view of the Vietcong and the North Vietnamese. No one mentioned this at the ordnance officer training.

These were politically infuriating times. The people responsible for the war were gone. Kennedy was dead. Johnson, after trying to win something, if not victory then at least a conclusion that looked like satisfaction, had given up. Johnson had lost the avuncular TV journalist Walter Cronkite's support, and he said that if he had lost Cronkite, he had lost the American people. The television news, probably more responsible for the start of the war than any other single factor, had turned solidly against more war. Luckily for Cronkite no one remembered that Cronkite himself, in the early years of the American activities in Vietnam, was very much in favor of patrolling Indochina and fighting communism. He reported almost gleefully from the battlefield with much praise for what the American boys were doing. So Johnson's fear that if he lost Cronkite he had lost the people was probably wrong. Cronkite got sick of the war because people were sick of it, and he had to get out ahead of popular opinion so as not to get blamed for his earlier support. It was pretty much a business decision.

Even then, though I didn't know exactly why, I could see that poor old Johnson had deceived himself. He thought the US could control what happened, and that was fallacious. He said, "We seek no wider war." Well, maybe we didn't, but the decision was pretty much out of our hands. Maybe we didn't seek a wider war, but the North Vietnamese were fine with a wider war. And so were the Chinese, and the Russians, and the Eastern Bloc of communist countries. And in a way so were the Thais who rented the US land for a huge airbase, and the Japanese, who sold tens of thousands of motorbikes to the Vietnamese and cameras to the GIs. And so did the construction companies who built harbors and roads in Vietnam, companies like RMK, partially owned and controlled by Lyndon Johnson's hideous wife, Lady Bird.

Friends now are aghast, or at least act that way, when I tell them of this period, and ask why I didn't just throw away my uniforms and head out for Canada. They ask if I could have done that. Well, I could have, or more exactly the person I am now could have done it. But who I was then couldn't, or at least didn't. It didn't occur to me as a real possibility. It was not only that I was young and easily pushed one way or another but also that I had been raised to think that the United States, while confused and harassed by events, was generally on the side of good. The history of World War II was sugared over for several generations after the victory over the Nazis and the imperial Japanese. We, the US, had won the war, almost single-handedly, according to what Americans were told. Scant mention was made of the Russian contribution to the defeat of the evil Germans.

I recently admitted to some liberal friends, when we talked about current politics, that I had voted for Richard Nixon. In an odd sort of back-looking judgment, they condemned me and found this revelation unbelievable. My political drawings and writings in recent years would make such an act seem to be impossible, shocking even. I tried to explain, but they weren't convinced. Didn't I see that Nixon had been lying about having a secret plan to end the war when he campaigned in 1968? Didn't I realize that he would do anything to avoid being the first president to lose a war? Couldn't I see that he was a calculating crook and possibly the worst president we had ever had, even though now that judgment has to be reconsidered?

No. I couldn't see any of that. First because I was young, and second because the choice was between Nixon and Hubert Horatio Humphrey, Johnson's yakety-yak vice president. So, forced to choose, I chose to believe that Nixon had a secret plan to end the war. We now know that it was so secret that even Nixon didn't know what it was. Still, it was plain that Humphrey would be more likely to continue Johnson's approach. Besides, for some reason I didn't like Humphrey. And in truth I didn't think Nixon was going to win. I liked Eugene McCarthy, but he seemed to lack energy, content to be surrounded by people who agreed with him, and they were no help. If anyone were to stop the entrenched pro-war politicians and businessmen, he would need to preach beyond the choir. And Eugene McCarthy didn't.

I began writing this memoir after a dinner conversation with some young people who seemed interested in what Vietnam meant and how we fought in such prolonged and bloody battles against people who were now making clothes they could buy at Banana Republic. They found it

amazing that the government could order young people, just like themselves, off to a war, under threat of prosecution and prison. They found it amazing that anyone obeyed such orders. Why wasn't there wholesale revulsion, if not at the war, then at least at the enforcement of such slavery? Wasn't that unconstitutional?

I was amazed they knew so little about the Vietnam War. It is glanced at in American high schools, relegated to political science courses in college, and ignored in current political journalism. The war itself is called a loss for the US, although the outcome was far more complicated and intricate than a simple loss. It is said that Americans are shallow thinkers, trained by advertising and the consumer economy to judge problems quickly in whatever way requires the least reading or analysis. This is true, and it is troubling. I didn't want to come across sounding sorry for myself, because I don't feel sorry for myself. In truth, being pressed into the military and sent to war was destabilizing, hot, miserable, lonely, and crazy. It was also, in an awful way, interesting. War is interesting if you can avoid getting killed, and don't mind loud noises.

The one dominant feeling of being in Vietnam was confusion, a confusion that increased with every assignment I was given. I began to think that either I was more sentient than my fellow soldiers or that they had somehow been brutalized or baffled into mental submission and their own survival mentality. My father had joined the army "for the duration." But in Vietnam the tour lasted one year. If you could stay alive one year you were sent home. The trick to getting home was to survive somehow, in any manner, avoiding any and all risks. And the concurrent trick for the army was to force us to take those risks. In addition to all that confusion, or maybe replacing the personal confusion in my mind, was an increasing sense that the government and the army were working against me. They were working to waste my time, get me killed, and at best turn me into a distrustful, resentful version of the hopeful person I had always been. The *Catch*-22 definition of the enemy is anyone who is going to get you killed. Many on your own side. Undrafted, I probably would have sacrificed gladly for the nation, for its history and traditions, and for what I had been told was the overall goodness of the country. But now everything that I had been taught was suspect, and my list of things to hate and distrust grew every day. Relations with civilians didn't improve, either.

I began to plan for the time to come after the war. While at Aberdeen Proving Ground, I decided that I would apply for a graduate school, law or journalism. I had loved working for newspapers while in college in Denver. I liked the people and the excitement and the daily output of judicial and political writing. I liked printing and typography and the pounding roar of presses, which in my own colorful thinking I compared to the resounding triumph of drums at the end of a symphony. That's a little bit of a stretch, but the daily intensity of getting the paper out was invigorating and seemed important.

I decided to apply to graduate journalism schools — Columbia and Northwestern. I took the train from Washington to New York for an interview with a dean, whose name, luckily for him, I have forgotten.

The Vietnam War was by that time so unpopular that almost no respect was paid to soldiers or veterans, so traveling in uniform was seldom done. But in uniform you got half-price fare on the trains. I got on the train in Washington's Union Station. Halfway to Baltimore the conductor informed me that if I hadn't bought my half-fare ticket at the station I had to pay full price. He said he couldn't give me the military fare on the train. Whether or not this was a real rule, I saw no reason why the military fare shouldn't be awarded on the train. I was serving the goddamn country, wasn't I? The conductor, a man with substantial girth, seemed cruelly amused by a situation in which he could annoy and inconvenience anyone, especially some young shit of an officer. I said I wouldn't pay.

The train stopped in Baltimore, and the discussion of my fare and the rule in question became heated. A variety of slurs, some impossible to retract, were exchanged. Other passengers took sides. The discussion became a screaming match, bellowsome, with some accusing the conductor of being little short of a commie, some accusing me of being obnoxious and a smart-ass, and probably a baby killer, some offering to pay the difference for my ticket. The conductor ordered me off the train. Like hell I said. Make me I said, you fat bastard. Some of my backers among the passengers thought this uncalled for, and certainly unbecoming an officer.

So the train sat there in Baltimore, unable to move without the conductor's approval. I knew I was screwing up everyone's travel schedule, but I didn't care. Worse than that, I perversely enjoyed being able to make my dissatisfaction with nearly everything and everybody into something real. After a short wait several Baltimore police officers came on the train, and the other passengers were treated to the sight Americans have grown accustomed to after things get bad enough — that is, Americans fighting with each other. But the police, like me in uniform, refused to do anything. The conductor refused to give up, and there we sat. Into this cauldron appeared a small man from the railroad, an unlikely savior, a ticket agent. He gave me a ticket, no charge, and thanked everyone for their patience. And the train moved on. You will remember that I was teetotal during my army years, but by the time I reached New York, I was sorely tempted to start drinking again.

The interview at Columbia Journalism School was a similar disaster. I had brought no civilian clothes so I was in uniform when I went to the Columbia campus to see the dean, who looked at me strangely. I wasn't thinking very clearly. The Columbia campus was a hotbed of anti-war activity. Students took over the president's office. Black and white students fought over the university's obviously racially prejudiced decisions in real estate and admissions. The New York police restored order only to see disorder erupt as soon as they left. The confusion grew violent, and the racial divide was, even for those times, surprising. Every day a new outrage bubbled up. Into this steaming mix I walked, not so much naive as uniformed and uninformed. The dean probably thought I was a practical joke. He treated me with a disdain and disapproval I could not understand. Columbia was an unhappy place, a very unhappy place. The dean could have been more human, but he wasn't.

Here was the truly unforgivable aspect of the war, at least stateside. American citizens, young and old, vented their frustrations with the conflict, the waste, the cruelty, and so on, by being as awful as they could to their own soldiers. At first, for me, and I think for my fellow draftees, this attitude was at least puzzling. The puzzlement, unexpected from a nation that had praised and rewarded the soldiers of World War II, turned into exasperation and then reciprocal disgust. It was my mistake to go for an interview in uniform, but I didn't know how offensive this was. I still thought that people in high academic ranks at an Ivy League school would know that the soldiers weren't actually enjoying the war and were wearing uniforms because they were trying to save a few dollars on a train ticket. But no one involved with Ivy League schools hangs on to a high opinion of Ivy League schools for very long. As I remember, the dean couldn't bring himself to say anything encouraging, or even shake my hand at the end of the interview.

The training for newly commissioned ordnance officers was six months at Aberdeen Proving Ground. Parts of the schooling were interesting, but Maryland was not.

The clotted summer heat was destructive to anything resembling happiness. We studied artillery pieces, ammunition, explosives, tanks and tank recovery, how to repair broken tank tracks, and, a part I liked, how to replace engines in lumpy old Korean-era three-quarter-ton trucks. The trucks were old Dodges. The engines were flathead sixes, ancient cast-iron monsters, inefficient but easy to understand. During this training we made a note to ourselves that at least car repair might be something useful in our post-military careers. Even at this desperately late date I can take rudimentary care of my car.

6

But an unforgivable thing was happening. As I tried to assimilate my new training, I began to forget all the Vietnamese I had studied. At first I tried to keep some words in my memory, reading through the lessons and my carefully made flash cards. This dedication didn't last long. I had developed an odd affection for things Vietnamese, the culture, the people, the history with all its invasions and colonial outrages. But to keep a language alive in your mind you have to have daily conversations, to be surrounded by advertising, and to read newspapers. On the eastern seaboard there were no Vietnamese restaurants, and none in Washington. None of the other officers at Aberdeen had any interest in Vietnamese, or my odd training so far. They were almost all ROTC reservists, with even less real interest in the army than I had. In time most of my facility in Vietnamese faded, although even today I can remember bits and pieces. And now Vietnamese restaurants are everywhere.

In short, the army, through sheer inadvertence or stumbling unconcern, was willing to let the year of language training disappear. The money spent on instruction and the money spent on me was simply not valued. It was wasted, like the greater portion of the war effort. Who cared? The army didn't. I didn't. Nor was it a secret that no one cared. At the highest level the concern was simply political preservation. Nixon wanted to avoid being the first president to lose a war, no matter what the cost. He was a soulless bastard, Nixon, who had one redeeming feature — he looked like what he was. He would say whatever he had to say about the defeat of communism and about the domino theory, but no one believed any of it. And the fighting went on.

I repeat myself. The initial reason for this narrative was my experience talking to young Americans who wanted to know what the period in American history was like. I was discovering that this was a delicate task. You want people, in this case people not affected directly, to understand something they are curious about but not necessarily interested in. You have to go slowly, sometimes telling several stories in parallel, sometimes ignoring small horrors like the self-immolation of Norman Morrison in front of the Pentagon. This is hard to believe. Yes, Norman Morrison left his young daughter with someone nearby and set himself on fire under the secretary of defense's window. Most young people today don't know that a man named Norman Morrison poured kerosene on himself and lit himself on fire where Secretary of Defense Robert McNamara could see him from his office.

And does this bear repeating? The total tonnage of bombs dropped on the North Vietnamese, Cambodians, and Laotians exceeded all the bombs dropped by all sides in World War II. Strange and almost unbelievable numbers and stories have to be explained so they can be understood and marveled at properly. The total of bombs dropped is pretty impressive if you know how many bombs were dropped in World War II. If you don't, it's just a passing statistic. And then there's the almost humorous irony that toward the end of the Vietnam War, the air force ran out of bombs and had to buy some back from the West German government.

During the year I was studying the duties of an ordnance officer, and while my language skills faded, the war went on and the nation rebelled against it. According to the army's statistics, we were killing more North Vietnamese than they were killing Americans. This was taken as proof of the efficacy of our tactics and strategy. And it might have proved something if the numbers had been accurate. But the numbers were fudged. No one, certainly not at the battalion level, wanted to admit that the daily contacts with the enemy were costing more American lives than they were costing the communists. To admit that would have had two unpleasant results. First it would have added to the towering dissatisfaction with the war. Second it would have raised doubt about the commanders on the ground. Commanders would have been relieved, which is army terminology for "fired," and sent home in shame. After all the work and sacrifice to become a division commander in a war zone, officers did not want to be relieved and humiliated.

To prevent this, officers simply had to provide numbers of enemy killed that were in excess of Americans killed. Lies about American deaths could not be sustained, but lies about enemy deaths could. The enemy died in the jungle, in thick mountain forests. Some floated away down rivers. The numbers of enemy killed in a skirmish or full firefight were conveniently uncheckable. So no one checked. Why should they? Many enemy deaths resulted from artillery attacks in which the bodies were often eradicated, exploded, liquidated.

The public face of the war, General William Westmoreland, let slip that he thought the American public would accept a weekly death toll roughly equal to the number of Americans killed on the nation's highways. This was a crude calculation that showed Westmoreland's dim understanding of politics. If the weekly war dead were held to an acceptable number all would be well. The only danger was the chance that Americans would suddenly begin driving more safely, in which case further adjustments would be made. Westmoreland might have convinced other politicians who very much wanted to be convinced. But his announcements didn't go very far. No one believed the announced number of enemy killed because in a larger, simplified sense no one believed anything. Platoon officers reporting the result of their firefights with the North Vietnamese were tempted, and in some cases encouraged, to add fictional casualties. Reports were turned in and went up the line. At the company level a few more enemy casualties were added, a few more at battalion, and so on. This temptation was safe because there was no way anyone could check. Dead Vietnamese in the jungle or floating down the Mekong had disappeared. And there was nothing amazing in this. People have always believed what they wanted to believe.

But after a time, the newspaper and television reporters tumbled to the fact that they were being lied to. The numbers were suspected to be fiction. Proof was demanded. By lucky coincidence the Polaroid company introduced a compact instant camera that held film for twelve instant pictures. After the shot was taken, the developed pictures came out of the front of the camera in mere seconds, in color and with decent focus. This seemed to be a solution to the problem of inaccuracy in reporting enemy dead. You had to have a picture of each reported kill. The Polaroid cameras were issued in great number to all platoon leaders, and they were taken into the jungle and the forest on patrols. The doubts would be answered.

Except that they weren't, because while other shortages were everywhere, there was no shortage of Polaroid film. Multiple pictures could be taken of the same dead enemy soldier. Back at the officers' club these extra shots could be traded to other platoon leaders, sort of like baseball cards. The unkind but inarguable fact was that one dead Asian boy looks pretty much like another, and besides, and this is the most important *besides* in the entire process, who cared? Not even General Westmoreland. Somewhere, I suppose, in the Pentagon's records of the war there are many boxes of Polaroid pictures of the communist dead, which could be reviewed for similarities. Unless, of course, these have been declared classified and destroyed.

The fighting continued. The bombing continued. Back at Aberdeen Proving Ground my ordnance training ended. I left with the same feeling most Americans have about life in the state of Maryland — nothing. I was assigned to a security staff operation at Fort Belvoir, Virginia, about twenty miles south of Washington, DC. In this job I would gain knowledge and experience of what newly commissioned officers did in a regular assignment. I would have some months of dealing with a command, implementing policy, doing staff work, writing reports, sitting in meetings, and conducting myself like an officer, whatever that meant. The army made repeated attempts to interest me in an army career. I was counseled about the advantages of being an officer: promotions, secure pay, health care, extra money for family members, and other advantages, such as very cheap movies at the base theaters. I smiled and said nothing. I had learned by this time that the way to deal with the army was to let it think it was getting what it wanted out of you. I listened to the career counseling with a practiced, quizzical look. I said I would think about it. The truth was that any attempt to interest me in an army career only proved the fact that the army was desperate for officers. The only way they could have gotten me to sign up for more time would be to guarantee no service in Vietnam. But that wasn't possible so I didn't even suggest it. At one point I said that I thought I wanted to go to law school, and I was immediately promised law school tuition and additional money. All I had to do was to sign up for more years — four to be exact.

The draft wasn't working. Thousands of young men ignored letters from their draft board. The cost to find them was as high as the effort to either make them into soldiers or lock them up. This grinding labor grew until it was not worth it, and the expense was clear not only to the government but also to the young men themselves. There were other ways of becoming undraftable. Some became priests or reverends, a classification that got them a pass. Some immediately got married and had children. Some stayed in graduate programs of no value. Some discovered that they were homosexuals, some feigned insanity, some committed crimes. In all sorts of ways, it became more difficult to find replacements for the returning veterans. News stories about this burgeoning problem spread the feeling of hopelessness and revulsion at the prospect of military service. In isolated instances, at least in news accounts, some young men injured themselves or decided to establish a history of drug or alcohol dependence.

The draft rules were changed so that it operated in an even more cowardly way than before, disguised as a lottery. Your birthday was drawn out of a hat and assigned a likelihood of being drafted. These numbers were then announced. It's hard to imagine a less intelligent method. After the numbers were announced those with low numbers fled to Canada or Sweden if they could afford to. If they couldn't afford to, they remained in the US and took their now increased chances, obviously even more incensed at their lousy luck. No one believed that the lottery drawing was done fairly.

At any given time in the late 1960s the army had around five hundred thousand men in Vietnam. Less than half of these were combat troops, but all were in harm's way. They were support staff, cooks, signal corps, medical staff, and so on. The risk of getting killed or wounded may have varied with the assignment or role in a normal war, but in Vietnam the only thing close to a front line was the perimeter of a firebase, a clearing in the jungle of a few acres surrounded by wire fencing and walls of sandbags. The usual firebase had three or four artillery pieces and a dozen mortars. But during the building of a firebase everyone was at equal risk, especially the engineers. It could be said that the infantry, out on patrol in the bush, were possibly safer, since no one knew exactly where they were. The firebase, like a fort, was plainly visible to everyone, detectable by its lights at night and flagpole during the day. Most American firebases made lots of noise: music, generators, and Americans yelling at one another. And the army allowed dogs, incredibly mangy mutts, to be brought in as a comforting factor, a reminder of life back home. Some of them howled all night.

But my overseas orders were delayed an additional six months. During this time, I did nothing at Fort Belvoir. Well, not completely nothing. I was forgetting whatever Vietnamese vocabulary was still in my head, but no one seemed to be bothered by that. It began to look as though my time stateside might actually outlast the war. The Paris Peace Talks had begun. Nixon talked about various aspects of his secret plan. I began to hallucinate that I would receive RIF orders — reduction in force — in short, a notice that they no longer needed me because peace had broken out. In retrospect such hallucinations are unexplainable other than being the product of a mind weakened by inaction.

Fort Belvoir, on the coast of Virginia, not far from George Washington's farm Mount Vernon, was the headquarters of the Corps of Engineers. You could say that the corps was the most unwarlike part of the army, more concerned with building bridges and roads in combat areas than in actual shooting at the enemy. Of course, while they were building bridges and roads they were shot at daily. This called for a special bravery and the ability to concentrate on the task at hand. In the continental US the Corps of Engineers' role included all sorts of dredging and dam building, for which they often got vicious criticism since dams fail and dredging is sometimes misunderstood. At Fort Belvoir, the Corps of Engineers took good care of themselves, especially in the construction of the officers' club.

The Corps of Engineers Officers' Club was a pleasure palace unequaled by any other officers' club, maybe anywhere in the world. It was built on a gentle escarpment of the eastern United States, sloping gracefully down to the Atlantic. There were swimming facilities, boat docks, dining halls, amusement areas for children, and repair sheds for officers' watercraft. Crowning the entire enterprise was the clubhouse, an enormous redoubt done in a mid-Atlantic architectural style with added unconvincing plantation ponderousness and the military libido for the squat.

I was expected to join and contribute to the club every month from my pay. I was not happy about this. I did not want to join or attend the endless list of functions, some expressly for young officers. I disliked the concept of command performance. For some of these I had to wear dress blues. Every service has its high dress uniforms, and the army's version are particularly awful — a style said to have been copied from the Revolutionary War uniforms but which had in the years since taken on the flamboyance of a headwaiter at the Budapest Howard Johnson. The colors were red and a sort of homely cobalt blue with shoulder boards and braiding and all sorts of other decorations and unnecessary brass hardware. Fill a room with men in these outfits, and the result is nothing short of comical.

I tried — in the usual weak-willed way I did everything else — to get out of the monthly expense for the officers' club and was told that this was not excusable. Joining and supporting the club was part of my commitment to being an officer, and that rank had its privileges even if they weren't wanted. I didn't really want to be an officer. My focus was on stalling. I would do whatever was necessary, but all this parading around in military finery, all this expense for special uniforms (which I had to rent), seemed to lose track of the reason I was ostensibly there in the first place: to beat back communist aggression in a country I had previously been unable to find on a map. Why couldn't I just get on with it and then go home? Or more desirably, just go home.

Even though I was losing my knowledge of Vietnamese at a steady rate, I still entertained the idea that if I were sent to the war zone, I would be safely placed at a desk reading captured enemy documents for intelligence clues. News footage from the war showed fighting reminiscent of the World War II operations in the South Pacific. My father had been in New Guinea and Tarawa as an anti-aircraft artillery officer. He talked very little about it, but he said he never got used to explosions or gunfire. His brief recollections combined with the Hollywood re-creation of jungle fighting made me cling ever more strongly to my version — me, sitting at a desk reading documents.

During my time at Fort Belvoir, I quite accurately did less than nothing. There was nothing for me to do. There were no documents in Vietnamese for me to translate. I was assigned to a part of the Corps of Engineers called the Combat Development Command. This sounded like something important, but it wasn't. Typically, the fact that it wasn't important but sounded important was important. One project stood out for wild creativity and endless expense. I can't remember the name of this project, but it involved methods of rapidly digging trenches so that defensive perimeters could be established in ground combat. If there was any combat foresight involved, it was the expectation that the US would be fighting the Soviet Union and the East Germans, and we would have to have trenches on the frozen East German border in a hurry to block an area known as the Fulda Gap. Soviet tanks would come streaming through, and trenches were the only defense. Then, after the Soviets were repulsed, more trenches would be needed. I sat through some briefings on the tactics to be used.

The heart of all this was the development of a vehicle that would dig trenches quickly, and in frozen tundra. This vehicle, mounted on tracks and fortified against anti-tank rockets, had a front blade-and-scoop affair with a set of heavy drilling nozzles. The nozzles would be driven into the frozen earth. Pumps forced a gasoline-and-air mixture into the earth, and some sort of spark plug ignited it. The frozen earth was exploded, casting enough material away so the vehicle could move forward and repeat this procedure. A drawback seemed to be that the vehicle itself, after a series of these powerful explosions, would begin to come apart at the seams. How long would the trench machine be operational after deployment, and how strong would it have to be? How could tests be conducted?

The money for these tests was lacking because of the great expense of the Vietnam War. Officers and Pentagon officials who had the bad luck to be assigned to development of the exploding trenching machine had little they could do but sit around writing reports in expectation that one of these days the funding would come through and careers could be continued. Meanwhile we could only hope that the Soviets and the East Germans wouldn't attack. I was assigned to make sure that in the slack waiting period our staff did not go soft physically. I was put in charge of a physical fitness program, which involved some paperwork and some scheduling. This touched everyone in the command. They had to show up for a routine of running and climbing over walls and doing pull-ups. Of course, if they were too busy to make my schedule of exercises, they could simply provide some documentation that they had done these exertions on their own time. I was given the power to decide if the documentation was convincing or merely a ruse. I excused everyone who outranked me, the older sergeants and officers, majors and above, who probably needed the exercise, and came down hard on the younger sergeants and second lieutenants, who probably didn't.

As my proficiency in translating Vietnamese faded, my skill at dealing with the army increased. I am not an abnormally devious person, and even if I were, the clear need for managing the people who had command over me would be obvious. I have heard this skill called back-managing, a practice in which you get those with authority over you to issue orders and policies of which you approve. In more subtle corporate situations this business is probably more difficult, but in a military venue it seemed to me to be fairly straightforward. The army and the other services claim they have a unique authority, not found in any other organization. This authority is command. Other organizations can tell you what to do, but you may or may not do it. You may decide that you will wait, or question, or ask for more guidance, or simply resign your job. You are not commanded to do some task under threat of jail or being hauled off to the nearest wall for execution. Command is simple on its face, but the definition is far more complicated. The danger is the assumption that command is something that it is not.

At least in the American army the concept of command is misunderstood because a great many people think that reality is the way it is portrayed in war movies. To make a war movie plot move along commands are issued followed by a warning, "That's an order" — something I never heard spoken in the States or overseas. Soldiers I knew quickly figured out that the orders were only as effective as the consequence of not obeying. If the result of not obeying was preferable to obeying, the order could go to hell. For most of the enlisted men in the lower ranks the result of disobeying an order might be dismissal from the service and being sent home. This dishonor and the resulting dishonorable or general discharge might have bothered men in some wars, but it was a minor consideration during the Vietnam War. Being thrown out of a military service and a situation you never wanted to be in in the first place had no particular shame. In addition, if the civilian population, especially the population in the age range of the draftees, thought the war was evil, stupid, illegal, and criminal, anyone expelled dishonorably might find praise back home. And some did.

You may remember that I was first assigned to Fort Dix, in southern New Jersey. There I first discovered how far army discipline fell short of what I had supposed it to be. I learned what being AWOL actually meant. Fort Dix was a large military installation with many thousands of trainees. And it is close to New York City, a place with innumerable holes in which to hide. A soldier who made up his mind to opt out of the war could find support in New York from friends, family, or antiwar groups. Most soldiers probably knew several of their fellow troops who just failed to return from a weekend pass, or just never showed up at an ordered transfer. Coupled with the opportunity to simply leave was the subtle reality of a draftee's relationship to the war itself.

This relationship was as follows: Most American males of draft age would have probably found the actual war interesting, even — and this is a stretch — enjoyable. Patrolling jungle trails, listening for a clever and resourceful enemy, shooting and attacking, winning medals, and so on, was something they had all done in their imaginations as young boys. The actual war itself was simply an extension of youth, if they were only allowed to get on with it. If you wanted a young American male to get going and shoot other boys, communists or whatever they were, or anyone else who was in the way, you only had to give him a gun and some ammunition, and he'd be off and at it in no time.

It was the army itself that was loathed. It was the standing in rows, the idiotic requirements, the being yelled at in an approximation of rage and forced to run in boots, the enforced respect for ranks, the prisoner haircuts, the belittling treatment from drill sergeants — who obviously were of severely limited intelligence — the days and weeks of wasted time, wasted effort, marching, stopping, waiting, memorizing things that made no sense, things that were the demonstrably archaic practices of previous wars, the enforced stupidity and the moronic consider-ations. It was the combination of all these things with no understandable object ahead. And even for those draftees lacking an adequate knowledge of history and sociology there was the debilitating feeling that they were caught in a huge, ponderous, uncaring, and unstoppable grinding machine with no one driving. So when a door opened to escape, or simply leave, many took the opportunity with-out a second thought.

How then did the army get people to do what it wanted them to do? To a large extent it simply didn't. In some cases it pretended that things were better than they appeared. It pretended that its training was effec-tive when it wasn't. It pretended that orders were obeyed when they weren't. It pretended that the resistance to the war had little effect when it was loud and powerful. And it continued to pretend that the army itself was convinced of the rightness of the mission in Southeast Asia, at the very same time the highest ranks were riddled with doubt.

I began to pay attention to all this disorganization and indirection while still at Fort Belvoir, carefully slipping sideways into discussions with other young officers about what the hell was going on. Most of these discussions were seeking support for the increasing doubtfulness we all felt. Again, we found examples of outright lunacy in our superior officers, certainly in those who remained steadfastly convinced that the US would come out of the war victorious. The most convinced were reserve officers, majors and lieutenant colonels, called up for a stint of active duty. I suspected that these temporary officers, insurance managers and midlevel corporate executives back home, had agreed to or sought active-duty service to relieve the tedium of their civilian jobs. Some were simply looking for or hoping for adventure.

In contrast, the officers with almost no conviction of the rightness of the war were the regular army officers. Many were from West Point. They had promised the army many years of service, and the army promised them the same in return. West Point cadets are taught political history, military history, including the way political and cultural mistakes get armies in trouble. I came to appreciate the education a student gets at West Point, including a strong introduction to reality. I never had any desire to apply to a service academy and probably would not have gone, even if accepted. But if they teach nothing else at West Point and Annapolis, they teach some hard truths. For example, they teach army cadets never to trust the air force.

The days were slow and almost meaningless. I spent free time biking around the city of Washington, spending time at the Smithsonian, the memorials, the Folger Shakespeare Library, the outer suburbs, and the wastes of DC's poor black northern areas. I sat in the House and Senate, sometimes hearing rationales for military operations that I later discovered were complete fabrications. It was a time when senators and congressmen often showed up and gave speeches drunk, and when spittoons still graced the floor.

Supposedly if I got down to around one year remaining in my promised time, the possibilities of being sent to Vietnam were much less, and the rumor was that there was no possibility of overseas orders if you owed less than twelve months. I showed up for duty, day-to-day, looking over my shoulder at the calendar. The coastal Virginia summer miasma settled, deadening the desire to do anything worthwhile. I befriended a fellow from northern Vermont who had reenlisted and bought a new Chevrolet with the bonus. He was amusing and didn't ask a lot from life. I can't remember how I met him, because he was a cook, an E5, in one of the Belvoir mess halls. He was cheerful and loved to drive his new car home for the weekend. It was a long, pounding drive, reaching Vermont around midnight at St. Johnsbury, where my wife would meet me. My friend the cook had been in hellish fighting in Vietnam, wounded three times. He laughed this off with a sort of rural toughness, pointing out that they tried but they couldn't kill him, and wasn't that amusing. The army declined to send him back to the infantry after three woundings, offering him what I thought was a crappy choice of being a drill instructor or going to cook school. He had enlisted to see more of the world than his home-town, a tiny Vermont village called Kirby, but after seeing the world, and getting shot three times, he just wanted to see Kirby.

We drove the nearly six hundred miles from Fort Belvoir to St. Johnsbury at as high a speed as we dared, beating his new car pretty badly. And then Sunday night we'd beat it back again to be there in time for Monday duty. He had to cook and be there early. I had to do nothing but sit behind a desk and wait for the day to end. In all this driving, however, we never grew close. He was still suspicious of officers and people with college degrees. As unobtrusively as I could I tried to ask him about his opinion of his experience and his relationship with the army. He would first give me a silly answer, broadly accepted enlisted humor, tough but self-deprecating. Beyond that, even when I got a little more incisive, he admitted that the army had probably been shitty to him and that he should have demanded more. And beyond that, he admitted that the war was stupid and worthless. Worst admission of all was that he really liked the Vietnamese people, and he was sorry to have shot some of them. There was a problem in our conversations, and it was that he associated the mission of whatever we were doing in Vietnam, whether worthwhile or plain rotten, as more my fault, as an officer, than it was his as just a soldier. I accepted this and didn't much like it. And the overall effect was that I resolved to be as ineffectual an officer as I could be.

But then, shit. When I was down to about fourteen months left, I got orders for Vietnam. I can remember being called into the colonel's office and handed the paper. I stood and stared at it. The colonel who ran the office waited for some sort of response, and I was determined that he wasn't going to get one. I simply gave him a noncommittal salute and thanked him. But later I stared at the paper and wondered what it actually meant.

I had to tell my wife, which was not going to be easy. But other complications were in wait.

My younger brother had been drafted after dropping out of college. He had applied for officer candidate school and had made it through, awarded a commission as an infantry officer. Not the world's most coveted commission. Infantry second lieutenants had the shortest life expectancy of any officer in Vietnam. They were assigned as platoon leaders and led patrols in the jungle. There was equal risk of being shot by the North Vietnamese or, if he pushed his platoon too hard, being shot by his own men. It's not too much to say that it was a jungle out there. My brother was a cheerful person, and he suffered from the twin characteristics of charm and carelessness. He probably would be greatly liked by his men, but that didn't mean he was safe. He was stationed in Texas, and his orders for Vietnam arrived at the same time as mine.

There is a general rule in the army, now known inaccurately as the Private Ryan rule, dating from the Second World War, which states in effect that two siblings will not be assigned to the same war zone at the same time. Private Ryan, at least in the Hollywood version, the story of which is almost totally contrived, was the last of four brothers, three of whom had been killed in the European Theater. Tom Hanks is sent to find Ryan before he is killed, which would have wiped out an entire generation of the Ryans. In this rule, there are equal parts concern for an unlucky family and concern for bad publicity. In a popular war like World War II, publicity was a secondary worry for the army. But in Vietnam killing off the oldest, me, and the second oldest, my brother, might involve bad press and congressional inquiry. I knew this, but my brother, in his perfected carelessness, wasn't worried.

I could have drawn attention to us both being on orders, but it was complicated. I was in a relatively safe, or so I thought at the time, role in the army. I still thought that my language skills would land me in a headquarters job in Saigon where the loudest noise would be the air conditioner. My brother, an infantry officer, would without doubt be on the ground going after the bad-tempered North Vietnamese, leading his equally bad-tempered men. In addition, I had a child by that time. My brother wasn't even married. To bring this to the attention of the army personnel people would be to ask for a decision that might put him at risk and spare me the war zone. We talked about this once briefly, and we decided . . . nothing. He had been through one tour in Korea and was by this time a captain, in helicopter school in Texas. He had found Korea duty dull and annoying, and probably would have welcomed the idea, if not the reality, of going to a shooting war. As I say, he was careless about many things, including himself. So we decided, and we did, the aforementioned nothing.

Someone in the vast reaches of the Pentagon personnel offices caught the fact that we both had been assigned to the war. They ordered him to a second tour in Korea and let my Vietnam orders stand. No one was happy, which is often the way the army likes it.

I had a two-week leave to get my things together, rent the house in Vermont, put the car in storage, and get my wife situated with her parents in Denver. She planned on finishing a master's program so the time would be used to some advantage. I got an issue of jungle fatigues and boots and loaded everything in an old duffel bag I found in the house and that still had my father's name stenciled on the side. We flew to Denver, saw some old friends, and spent a night at the Brown Palace Hotel. The conversations were stilted and pretty much ignorant of what was happening. There was a small gathering at the airport to say good-bye to me. And then I left.

7

On the plane, after it was clearly too late to do anything about anything, I was almost impressed at how little I understood of what I was doing. I was not depressed. My ignorance of my situation, at least of the reason for my situation, was almost like some sort of ether. The first flight was to San Francisco, and there I boarded a contract airline to Saigon, Air America or Flying Tiger or some company with a lucrative Pentagon contract to deliver soldiers to the war. There were stewardesses, and they smiled but didn't make a lot of eye contact. There were no movies on the plane. And almost no conversation. If there was a common emotion among the soldiers it was one of failure. Somehow, we had been stupid enough to get caught in this trap. We were in an unfolding misfortune that we should have done something about years ago.

Any number of soldiers, draftees and otherwise, simply did not show up for their port calls. This was a serious infraction, punishable with imprisonment for something like desertion or cowardice or a combination. But if you really wanted to fail to report for your flight to Vietnam, you could disappear into a city, or to Canada, or Mexico, or Sweden, or to any one of the many countries that had declared their opposition to the Americans' war in Southeast Asia. Rumor had it that France and the Nordic countries would welcome American deserters and help them get situated. As usual, people believed what they wanted to believe. More intriguing than that was the rumor that the young women of those countries thought highly of Americans who had obeyed conscience and taken great risk to protest the war. Their approval was demonstrated eagerly. Knowing, or assuming, all that, you could feel at least sad and sorrowful sitting on a plane to Saigon, rather than to Stockholm. Sad and sorrowful, and in many cases, foolish.

The flight stopped in Hawaii, and we had a five-hour wait. To make sure no one acted on their doubts, we were kept in a separate part of the Honolulu Airport. Thoughtlessly, this holding tank had a view of part of the rest of the airport. From there we could see American vacationers and their children, all kitted out for fun in the sun. When they chanced to stop and look at us, there was no evidence that they appreciated our efforts to defend their way of life and ensure that they could continue being free from the scourge of communism. Some were men about draft age.

The army had faced a cataclysmic fall in morale by that time. Morale is not an afterthought in the American army as it might be in more brutal armies. The Russians, for example, in the Great Patriotic War, positioned units behind the forward units to make sure that no one tried to retreat. Stalin joked that it took a brave man to be a coward in the Soviet army. The American military did not do that. Americans willingly fought to defend the country and the way of life. We put ourselves on the line because we believed in democracy. Or so the popular notion held. But still, given the opportunity to include any number of small acts that would have made people feel a little better or a small degree more appreciated, the army failed. It chose to add any little degree of thoughtlessness it could think up.

On the plane the finance corps collected any money you had and replaced it with military scrip. No US money was allowed in Vietnam, a policy based on the fear that it would add to wartime inflation. The finance corps lieutenant came down the aisle collecting money and issuing scrip, all in paper, down to paper five-cent bills. The bills featured illustrations of a nuclear submarine on one side and the moon landing on the other. This exchange added to the already miserable feeling that things were changing for the worse. I didn't like it, but I accepted the situation and handed over my money. Others on the plane objected and three or four fights broke out between the finance corps lieutenant and the soldiers. I didn't know exactly what these fights on the plane meant, fights between men supposedly involved in the same mission, to control the spread of whatever it was. It could have been handled better, but it wasn't. The American money said IN GOD WE TRUST. The military scrip left that off.

At points during any wartime experience there are subtle hints at what the real power structure is. Your rifle is stamped with the name of the manufacturer, Colt or Remington; your C-rations were made by some contract outfit in Arkansas; your fatigues were stitched together in Alabama; and your boots were made by the lowest bidder for a contractor in Pennsylvania. You are being paid nearly nothing, but everywhere else someone is making

money. And then there are the aircraft and military vehicle manufacturers, sidelines for the mammoth commercial manufacturers. Ford made all the jeeps, Chrysler made the trucks, and Bell made the helicopters. I knew how the prices were structured. All the costs to make these things were added up, and then a set profit was added as a fixed percentage. So to make more money the manufacturer increased its costs. The excuse was the emergency or exigency of war in which the government and the nation needed a great many things in a hurry to ensure victory. But of course, Vietnam was not like that. The only victory being pursued with a sense of urgency by that time was Richard Nixon's reelection.

Still, a portion of us, from New York anyway, were a little shocked to see a huge sign at Tan Son Nhat Airport in Saigon when we deplaned that said YOU HAVE A FRIEND AT THE CHASE MANHATTAN BANK. We were either conscripts or soldiers of misfortune, and we didn't have many friends. But at least the Rockefellers liked us.

The first days in country were spent in some last-minute training to explain that all the training you had received back in the States was wrong. So wrong, in fact, that it might even get you killed. We were given several days of retraining with weapons and shown the major failings of the M16 rifle. The M16 was designed to be light enough for the smaller Vietnamese troops to carry, with many of the parts — the stock and the barrel grip —made from plastic. It was the most unconvincing weapon ever designed. The rounds were only slightly larger than a .22 bullet although of much higher velocity. To make up for the poor design, a panic plunger had been added to the earliest models. The precision was too high for jungle fighting, so that when used in the rain, or dropped in a rice paddy, they often jammed. The panic plunger provided a second chance to force a new round into the chamber. The Vietnamese soldiers, who turned out not to be too small and weak to carry a heavier weapon, preferred Kalashnikovs, the Russian-made 7.62 mm rifles, made with far less precision but unaffected by water.

We were exposed to explosions so we could distinguish between incoming mortars and outgoing artillery. I became friends with another officer, a scared-to-death doctor whose name I recall was Bczyk. Dr. Bczyk was in the army because the Pentagon had helped him pay for medical school and he promised them some years in return. But Dr. Bczyk, a disastrously tremulous fellow, was not cut out for wartime duty. Explosions of both kinds — mortars and artillery — made Dr. Bczyk become extremely nervous; in fact he became almost totally destabilized, barely able to stand. In his destabilization he gripped my hand and buried his head in my chest. He was very embarrassed, and on one terrible occasion, after taking his first anti-malaria pills, beshat himself. I helped him to get cleaned up, not feeling at all continent myself. We had begun the yearlong ingestion of quinine pills and para-quinone pills that turned one's bowels to uncontrollable liquid. Whether this prevented malaria I don't know.

I told one of the trainers during these first days that I thought Dr. Bczyk should be reevaluated and perhaps kept away from explosions. But I don't know if my comments were at all helpful. Wherever Dr. Bczyk is now I wish him luck. Besides his odd name and unmilitary bearing, he also wore his hat with the bill off to one angle. All I remember with any accuracy is his head buried in my chest, gripping me during the exposure to explosions. I am pretty sure he was weeping. After those first four days I never saw him again.

My theory that I would be assigned to some safe and comfortable offices at the army headquarters or the American consulate, translating documents, was soon put to the test, and it failed. Nothing in the folders of orders I carried with me made any mention of the language school, or any of my enlisted service. I was an ordnance officer and was almost immediately assigned as an executive officer to an ordnance detachment of about two hundred men, part of the 1st Cavalry Division, at a base near Tay Ninh, north of Saigon and close to the Cambodian border.

The major task of the detachment was replacing artillery tubes on firebases. After a number of firings the tube of the gun became worn and slightly expanded by the explosives driving the shells. This altered the accuracy of the gun, a very undesirable effect. The artillery batteries fired hundreds of shells every day at targets called in by infantry units out in the jungle. The angle of elevation and the degree of azimuth were critical, as was the amount of explosive propellant placed behind the shell itself. Worn tubes meant shortfalls, often very close to the Americans who had called in the targets. There were instances when artillery batteries had hit American troops. This was a very bad thing to happen. It made the infantry units hesitant to call for artillery until they were well out of the way, and it made the artillery units add extra distance to the target to be sure they didn't kill Americans. With all these corrections and safety measures, chances were that the enemy, wherever he had been, was not there any longer. There was one way to correct for all this inaccuracy, and that was to shoot lots of shells. Maybe hundreds for a target that could eventually be hit with a few dozen. The one factor the enemy, both the Vietcong and the North Vietnamese, respected was American artillery. Even if not accurate, it was plentiful. The term *carpet bombing* was not applied to artillery, but it could have been. Our artillery was noisy and scary, even if not accurate.

To replace the gun tubes my detachment had to fly by helicopter to the firebases with new tubes, replace the old tubes, and fly back. The tubes were slung under the helicopter, and sometimes the whole gun was replaced. An entire 105 mm gun could be airlifted by a Huey. Sometimes the gun, hanging on an arrangement of straps, would begin swaying back and forth after we were up in the air, pulling the helicopter this way and that. I asked if there was any emergency disconnect so that if the weight of the

gun and the swaying was endangering us, we could just drop the damn thing and save ourselves. No one, it seemed, had thought of that.

My mechanical mind thought that an emergency disconnect arrangement, an explosive bolt, or some kind of solenoid gizmo that would cut the gun loose and save the passengers was not just helpful but mandatory. Two terrifying thoughts struck. First was that there was no way of dropping a gun and saving us. Second was that the people who should have thought of this, hadn't. Why hadn't they? And what else hadn't they thought of? This realization aroused a desperate anxiousness in me. The rest of the army seemed to accept a sloppiness and care-lessness that others have noted is an American failing. In short, since we are convinced that God is on our side, details don't count. God would take care of the details.

So within the first weeks in country I was flying back and forth to firebases, half in amazement and half in terror. In addition I had to somehow not show the interior terror, a task that requires an extra effort. Sometimes the terror was pushed aside by the amazement I felt toward the machinery of the pieces and parts of how the war worked. For example, a helicopter, which is, I will admit freely, an amazing machine. The principle of flight is turned into a precise rotary tool. You think about this and you are amazed. And then you think about the actual machinery involved. The blades are spun around and have their angle adjusted by one, rather small, intricate bearing that is powered by the jet turbine engine. The entire weight of the helicopter hangs on this extremely complicated machinery, rotating at a blinding speed. Between life — that is, getting home safely with the crew to live another day — and screaming death from three thousand feet with your life passing before your eyes, there's just this whirling, spinning metal hub, designed and produced by the same American engineers with the same unproven hope that God was on our side.

It doesn't pay to think about these things, certainly not with all the other dangers in a war zone — mortars, mines, incoming rifle fire, rockets, and sappers. In the time not spent in actual fighting you should be able to think about your family, your children, your future and their future. Reality interrupts when rank stupidity and nonsense is presented by commanders who deny the general lunacy of the situation. It took me about two weeks to begin an increasingly self-centered attitude. I would ignore idiotic orders and obey my inner coward, and if challenged I would freely admit this attitude. I heard one enlisted man respond to a major yelling at him about a mistake: "Sorry, sir, this is my first war."

8

Obviously, some people, men for the most part, want to be
soldiers, want to fight, want to prove their mettle (whatever mettle is) and enjoy competitive violence. These
people start wars. The rest of us are left to finish them. In
the case of the Vietnam War the initiators were largely the
US Air Force. When pressed, and even when not pressed,
and even when told to shut up, I could recount the historical failings of Eisenhower, Kennedy, Johnson, and Nixon.
In the decade after the Second World War, the US Air
Force told the politicians that Soviet and Chinese communist expansion could be controlled surgically from above
with something called, fingers crossed, strategic bombing.
If an insurgent force, like the Vietcong, for instance,
attempted to take over a democratically elected government, they could be bombed into retreat. This was
because being bombed was such a horrific, frightening,
unbearable experience that rebels would not want to challenge it a second time. Certainly not a third.

Except that this is complete crap, proven in every war
since the Blitz. Bombing raids must be followed by troops
taking over a ruined city or desperate countryside and
holding it. Bombed people are twice as angry as they
were before. Young men whose fathers you have killed

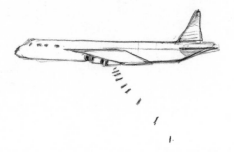

are now resolved to fight you to their own deaths. Fathers whose children you have killed are your sworn enemies forever. They are willing to die to get revenge. It was a repeated maxim that Asians did not revere and value life as much as Americans did. More crap, not tested and not proved. We could not control rebellions or communist insurgencies by dropping bombs on people. Historical examples were so numerous that only by resolutely ignoring history could anyone conclude that strategic bombing would work. To resolutely ignore this evidence, we had the air force.

Sometime in the 1950s the air force, no longer a part of the army, developed a concept known, either officially or jocularly, as the Air Force Plans for Peace. These plans were developed to counter the equally unproven theory that intercontinental ballistic missiles could keep people in line. For the air force the challenge was to keep the need for manned aircraft alive. If missiles were accepted as effective, why would jet fighters and huge bombers be needed? Why would anything other than missiles be needed? For a time John Kennedy was at least partially convinced that this was true. Fear of obsolescence ran through the upper ranks of the air force. Bombing would work. Especially nuclear bombing.

And then reality raised its ugly, grinning head. Bombing did not stop enemy insurgents. In fact, it gave the enemy the one thing they desperately needed, an enemy. Being bombed by the capitalist Americans meant, among other things, that Lenin, or Mrs. Lenin, was right. In World War II bombing didn't defeat the British, but never mind that, either. In fact, the air force concluded that the example of the Blitz could be used to make their point. Bombing did not defeat the British because, wait for it, Göring stopped too soon. Well, there, you see? He didn't bomb enough. That was his problem. We Americans would not make that mistake. Not us! We learned from history.

Bombing would work, the air force said, if you did it long enough. With this lesson from history firmly in mind, the Air Force dropped a tonnage of bombs on North Vietnam, Laos, and Cambodia so great that they, even today, cannot calculate it accurately. The popular claim is that the tonnage exceeded the total of all bombs dropped by all sides in World War II, but as previously asked, that means exactly what? Flying from bases in Thailand, the air force loosed hundreds of thousands of tons of bombs on the supply lines coming down through the jungle from the north, the Ho Chi Minh Trail. In theory, without supplies the North would capitulate. And maybe it would have, if the supplies were being transported on railroad trains. But the supplies, food, ammunition, medicines, and so on, were being transported on bicycles. The air force hadn't thought of that. They were dropping bombs on bicycles. Their theory was that the powerful and destructive American bombs would convince the North Vietnamese to stop fighting and give up. The bombing went on, year after year. The failure obviously was not bombing enough. Assurance was given that with another year of bombing, with more plentiful, more explosive bombs, the North would capitulate. They are a simple people, not very bright you see, and they are slow to get the point.

But in fact, they did get the point. The bombs raining from the sky proved that their leaders, Ho Chi Minh, General Giap, and others, were right. The Americans were the same as the French before them. They sought Vietnam's wealth, whatever it was, and they would, like the French, corrupt the government and enslave the people. It had nothing to do with communism. And like the French, the Americans could be defeated. The day would come when the Americans would pack up and leave. The indisputable fact was that bombing didn't bring victory in populated urban areas, and it was even less effective in the thick mountainous jungles of North Vietnam, Cambodia, and Laos. Anyone in the Pentagon could have figured this out, and perhaps they did, but it was never admitted.

In *Heart of Darkness*, Joseph Conrad early on describes a European warship firing a cannon at the African coast. There is a loud noise and a puff of smoke and the cannon-ball disappears into the huge, dark immensity of Africa. All to no effect. No one is impressed except maybe the gun crew on the ship. There is a loud noise and an echo, and then the silence returns, unchanged. Conrad was showing that what impressed the Europeans as superiority in weapons actually had no effect against the vastness of the African continent. It was similar to what the American bombing accomplished. It could not lead to victory, and it actually contributed to the chances of American defeat.

A bomb falls and explodes in the jungle, a ferocious roar, tons of dirt fly up in the air, trees are knocked over, the air is shocked. Fifteen seconds later the dirt has come down to earth, the trees lie there, and the stillness returns. Anyone not within about two hundred yards of the explosion is unhurt. A bit dazed perhaps, but free to march on. Not only has the explosion been ineffectual, but it has also dug a hole deep enough to be a fine shelter for the next attack. The bomb craters were just about everywhere after years of bombing. Thus, there were plenty of handy places to take cover. And how would a North Vietnamese on the ground know that it was time to take cover? No mystery there, either. The bombers, mostly B-52s, made lots of noise. They could be heard approaching, and thus gave warning that it was time to jump into the shelter provided by the previous bombs.

Certainly, some enemy were killed by US bombing. But the Ho Chi Minh Trail was nearly a mile wide in some places. If anyone with a logical military mind had added up the pluses and minuses of the nearly ten-year bombing campaign, they would have concluded that it was a failure. That conclusion could have been reached sometime well before the Tet Offensive in 1968, when the Americans and their South Vietnamese allies were surprised and pushed back by weapons and explosives brought down the Ho Chi Minh Trail quite safely.

Shortly after I arrived and was assigned to the ordnance detachment, the US command in Saigon decided to make a major incursion over the border into Cambodia. No one paid any attention to protests from the Cambodian government, which was as close to no government as possible. The leader, as far as anyone could see, was Prince Sihanouk, who seemed to be the last of a questionable royalty. Prince Sihanouk added a touch of comedy to an already tragic series of events. He was short and rotund, with a squeaky voice and a series of idiotic explanations of Cambodia's role in the war. The US incursion was to find a North Vietnamese supply depot of stuff brought down the trail. The North evidently planned to use the items in a full-scale onslaught against the Saigon area. The depot, called Rock Island East, was an enormous accumulation of weaponry, Chinese rifles and machine guns, Russian mortars, rockets, mines, and grenades. And bicycles. Thousands of Chinese-made bicycles that were used to transport the weaponry south, and then were of no further use. My detachment followed the mechanized US infantry up the highway and over the border.

Back home Nixon explained the significance of this operation on national television. His explanation was later revealed to have gotten it all wrong. His misinterpretation and his confused performance before a map was amusing enough in itself. Nixon had scant knowledge of Southeast Asia, and I believe little interest. Nixon relied on a man, I guess, named Henry Kissinger, his national security adviser at the time. Kissinger was a great sack of unwarranted self-regard who had Nixon in a trap. When his errors were later pointed out, there was cause for embarrassment. So the Nixon administration came up with the excuse that it had intentionally told the American people an erroneous tale because the enemy would be watching and might gain from an accurate rendition. Kissinger had the special intellectual skill needed to come up with such face-saving explanations. It was a misplaced skill without doubt, but still, in its perversity, special.

I traveled with a convoy of sorts north from Tay Ninh and over the border to Rock Island East. We would destroy any weaponry that couldn't be carried back to Vietnam. Somehow in the confusion of my assignment it had been assumed that, like most ordnance officers, I had some skill in explosive demolition. I did not. I was not qualified as EOD, explosive ordnance disposal. The very idea was scary enough, but that an army screwup had put someone, me, who knew nothing about explosives in a position to actually do something with explosives was frightening.

I came back across the border to Vietnam with the 15th Transport Battalion in heavy-duty off-road stake-and-platform trucks full of the collected weapons, Chinese rifles, mortar tubes and shells, rockets, hundreds of

thousands of rounds of rifle ammunition, and thousands of Chinese bicycles. I wondered, why not leave the bicycles? We could have given some of them away to the villagers, but no one gave such orders. The villagers watched us go by, nearly invisible in the clouds of dust. This huge volume of weaponry had been transported down the trail, on dirt tracks, through jungles and forests, across rivers, and all under daily bombardment by the air force. Anyone who gave this some analytical thought would conclude that these people, the North Vietnamese in particular, would be hard to beat.

What happened to all the weapons and matériel brought back from Cambodia in this huge operation was unclear. Some was donated to the South Vietnamese army, but I suspected that they wouldn't want it. They already had great amounts of American armament. In all probability it was mostly sold in some Saigon market and, in additional probability, sold back to the Chinese. Rumors, logical rumors, of wild corruption were traded everywhere. All were impossible to trace but easy to believe. By 1970 stories about failures of American planning and execution were valued by journalists and their editors back home much more than tales of heroism or success. After the 1968 Tet attacks, reports of failures were believed and reports of successes were not.

As the war went on, American commanders increased their distrust of the Army of the Republic of Vietnam, the ARVN, our allies. With good reason. The top ARVN officers had their positions because of cronyism and family connections. Even if some ARVN commanders had their positions because of military skills and bravery, Americans felt they were poor commanders. In the early years of the war, the American role was called an "advisory" one. Based on the US's overwhelming military superiority, from the Second World War on, the presumption was that we could help an ally by advising in tactics and strategy, but not actually getting into firefights. At times we would help with weapons and training, and strategic bombing, and maybe even some road and bridge construction. It's easy to see how this role could expand. In addition, the term *advisory* had more value as a way of gaining approval from the American government. Congressmen could more easily explain that the sons and daughters of their constituents were going to Southeast Asia to advise, in a friendly, avuncular way, rather than actually killing people.

The more important of the two US command structures in Vietnam was MACV, the Military Assistance Command in Vietnam. This bureaucratic mass of personnel was stationed near Saigon in a huge agglomeration of buildings, all air-conditioned and well PX'd. It had pools and gyms, and card rooms, and numerous officers' clubs. MACV headquarters duty was as luxurious as a war has ever been.

But the second command structure was USARV, the US Army in Vietnam. It was the regular American army, somewhat separate, and it kept its own counsel not only from its Vietnamese allies but also from MACV. The American army and the South Vietnamese army seldom shared intelligence. There were numerous examples of valuable foreknowledge about enemy operations and locations that the USARV developed but did not willingly share with anyone. Not even MACV. Why? The first reason was that it didn't trust the advisers because they were too close to the ARVN. Officers in the ARVN had ulterior motives — family connections, property to protect, infighting for promotions, and mutual distrust of the Americans. The second reason was a good deal worse — the Americans' lack of knowledge of the history of Vietnam. The American advisers either didn't know the country's history or didn't care. But the officers of the ARVN did. They knew that Vietnam had been at war somewhere or with someone for nearly all of its existence. The American phase of this constant state of war would come to an end. In the minds of ARVN officers and Vietnamese officials, it would be much less than a victory for the American allies, probably a stalemate, and possibly a defeat. So where then was the motivation to risk anything, lives, limbs, or anything of value?

I was assigned for a time as an adviser, helper, liaison, whatever I chose to call it, to the 9th ARVN Division. This assignment was only a marginal improvement over my role as an ordnance officer, and thankfully it only lasted about a month. The living conditions were actually worse than I had in Tay Ninh. Certain technological improvements were lacking. Rat traps, for example. The ARVN had none. The bunkers were full of large rats and other Asian specialties. The ARVN troops waged a battle against the rats by leaving out food and then shooting the rats that showed up to eat. Isolated shots rang out in the night, making sleep impossible. Sleep was impossible anyway, so there was little to effectively justifiably complain about.

My brief role with the ARVN was to accompany them on patrols, which I hated, to evaluate what weapons they needed. The evaluation was pretty simple. They needed everything. Then my job was to assist in the turning over of artillery pieces, trucks, jeeps, radios, and so on, to certain units. For reasons unknown, careful records were required. In the confusion of a war zone, mixed in with the heat and mud, the danger and the constant interruptions for fighting, exact records were difficult, and besides, and this is important, no one cared whether the records were exact. If a truck was taken from an American unit and transferred to a Vietnamese unit, even a move facilitated and witnessed by Lieutenant Danziger, whose sharp eye missed nothing, some sort of record was needed, not for the Vietnamese necessarily, but for the American unit that was losing a valuable property. It often amazed me, not that few people cared, but that anyone cared. There were army regulations to make them care. When a new commander came to a unit, he had to assume ownership of all the property of his new unit. Anything that was lost, destroyed, stolen, or simply not findable had to be covered in paperwork. There was little faith in any of the army's actual procedures, but there was great faith in paperwork.

Paper covered sins of omission, commission, and just regular old missions.

In my quite powerful job approving transfers of fairly expensive things like 105 mm howitzers, 175 mm howitzers, M113 tracked troop carriers, trucks, jeeps and mules, and even a few tanks, I did things as close to exact as I could. But that was not very. Large, maybe even huge, amounts of stuff were taken from American units and given to the South Vietnamese. Along the line, while I signed off on this stuff — including refrigerators, mobile army surgical hospital (MASH) units, radios, radars, tents, field kitchen equipment, cameras, and tons of metal roofing — it was observed that the donating American units were still there in the war zone, being shot at and mortared, but now without their stuff. The war was still going on. The secret plan to end the war, promised by Nixon, was still secret, except for certain parts. It was a major piece of cynical stupidity, but that was top secret.

9

In telling this sad story, full of waste and loss, I have been advised by friends and my own reading to add a touch of levity every so often. Does anything funny happen in a war zone? Well, yes, of course, as readers of numerous black-humor novels will know. Americans are ready to laugh at themselves, and sometimes it keeps them sane. We are a strange people, and we resist being forced into military structures. Which brings me to the requirement to shave every day. Bill Mauldin, the famous cartoonist in the *Stars and Stripes* newspaper, entertained the troops during the Second World War with depictions of his gloomy, war-weary, unkempt, and unmilitary semi-heroes Willie and Joe. Willie and Joe also needed a shave and clean uniforms. General Patton, despite his glorious Hollywood depiction, thought all his soldiers should be shaved, uniforms clean and pressed as they went to their foxholes. Patton was insane, as later proved, living in that same movie version of himself. But his legacy in Vietnam was a requirement that soldiers be barbered and that their boots be shined. This was considered to be an aid to morale. It was actually an aid to the conclusion that you were in an idiotic organization with almost no connection to reality. Why an infantry soldier needed to be free of facial hair could not be answered. Maybe the requirement was enforced just to see if people would do what they were told even if it made no sense.

Out in a tropical jungle for days on end, sleeping in hammocks and eating little tins of preserved tasteless-ness, drinking water that had a chlorine tinge, and spend-ing these days in the same clothes, filthy and sweaty, threatened by attacks from a ghostly enemy and shortfalls of your own artillery — all this was not good for morale. But why should you have to shave? Who cared? Who besides the army, whose commanders, at least majors and above, had living conditions where it was possible to lather up every morning. But there was always American ingenuity. Sometime in the middle years of the war, the Gillette company produced a clever aerosol can of shav-ing foam that contained chemicals that heated them-selves when combined. What it did to your skin was another matter. The product was called The Hot One, a whimsical touch from the Gillette marketing depart-ment. It was sold everywhere, especially in the army PXs in the war zone. You squeezed a gob into your hand and paused. Immediately the gob began to expand and steam. It became almost too hot to hold, and then it was ready to smear on your face. War movies should include the image of a soldier standing in the morning rain, in noth-ing more than an olive drab towel, smearing this triumph of chemistry on his face and trying to shave with a tiny mirror. Anyway, that's the funny part, and even the soldier in question, me, found it bitterly laughable.

By 1969, when the transfer to the Vietnamese of mili-tary goods began, the drawdown of American troops still hadn't begun. The effect that this clumsy plan had on the

already submerged American morale was pretty serious.
Items that were obviously necessary were hard to get.
American infantry units never completely refused a patrol
assignment, but they tailored the exact requirements.
How, for example, could you order men out on patrols,
searching for the enemy, without working radios? Radios
needed batteries, and often the batteries had either been
given to the ARVN or were still in the supply lines somewhere. A patrol should take two radios at a minimum.
Patrol units had to call for artillery or medevac helicopters. If batteries were not available the patrol assignment
was semi-suicidal. And the area that should have been
patrolled was much safer for the enemy.

None of these messes, these confusions, these screwups,
was invisible to the infantry. Ground troops in Vietnam,
condemned for not having the intellect or the money to
get into college and avoid the draft, or the proclivity in
Romance languages to get into the language school, could
still figure out that more care should have been taken to

boost their chances of getting back from a patrol unshot. Out in the forests and jungles, where the patrols actually went, the decision of what to do next devolved from the officer in charge to a sort of group decision, a subject for discussion rather than sharp-edged obedience.

On one trek with the infantry I observed a total reassignment of command from the lieutenant in charge to the group as a whole. I observed this because I, despite heroic efforts to not be there, was there. In the so-called free-fire zones, the native woodcutters operated at substantial risk. Woodcutting is a risky business during peacetime, but in the middle of marauding troops, searching for and shooting at each other, it is probably the worst job in the world. The plan was to find the woodcutters and talk to them to see if they knew anything or had seen anything. I was sent along with an infantry patrol who were already the veterans of several months' fighting and many contacts with the enemy. They regarded me as a strange addition to their patrol. We located a group of woodcutters strapping a monstrous mahogany tree trunk, at least thirty feet long, onto an ancient Renault diesel truck. The truck was in two parts. One end of the log was on the tractor, and the other end was on an axle. Chains and ropes and cables held the whole thing together. After a short talk, in which I understood only that nobody knew anything, the truck was started and crept off down the muddy track. And we were still there, having accomplished nothing. What to do?

A confab was held between the infantry troops and their lieutenant. Maybe there was enemy in the area, and maybe there wasn't. Did we care enough to try to search

for them? The radio operator reported back that we were still there. We were told to go on cloverleaf patrols. This meant setting a central point and then going out in four directions in circular routes looking for enemy. The lieutenant said he understood. Everyone approved, the men, the lieutenant, and, I suppose, me. Except that we didn't go out on cloverleaf patrols. We just sat down and let the time go by. I remember clearly that the lieutenant was an odd combination, quite distinctive — an Irish kid from Venezuela with a jovial attitude and flaming-red hair. He explained to me that we would not go looking for trouble, and in return we expected the same courtesy from the North Vietnamese. I said nothing, though it occurred to me that he was Irish and should have trusted cloverleaf patrols. This must have been sometime in December, because the lieutenant had brought along Christmas cards for his men to make out with a Christmas message to send to the division commanding general.

After about two months of duty in Vietnam as a translator/ordnance officer/whatever, I realized the many dangers of such duties. My plan to avoid patrols with the infantry had failed. My plan to get a secure job at MACV headquarters had also failed. I sat down and decided to do something about it. Among other annoyances was that I spent a full year cramming my head full of Vietnamese vocabulary only to have it wasted without so much as an apology.

I wrote a letter to my senator. I had never done this before, or, now that I think of it, since. I said that after a year learning Vietnamese, I was first assigned to mechanical maintenance, replacing gun tubes. In stern but respectful tones, I wondered if, as a taxpayer, I could complain about this obvious waste of funds. As a complaint it was bullshit, but as I previously mentioned, the army creates a fondness for bullshit. In truth I didn't care at all about the waste of taxpayer dollars. The waste of taxpayer dollars was the last thing the army worried about. Still, it seemed to sound like a legitimate political complaint. I put the letter in an envelope and stuck it in the mail, assuming that I would never hear anything about it, ever.

The portion of my screed about waste in the army in Vietnam was actually not bullshit. Waste in a war is inevitable, and it is tragic. The Pentagon, the army, or whoever made decisions bought all sorts of insane stuff that they must have known was not going to make a difference. For example, they bought thousands of plastic plants with radio transmitters in them. These were dropped from helicopters in areas where enemy troops were thought to be traveling. The plastic plants had pointed weights on the bottom so they would stick in the ground. When they detected human perspiration they would send a radio beep, a message that could be plotted on a map. Then the location could be patrolled with troops, or more likely shelled by artillery. The manufacturer had passed enough tests back in the US to get a contract for a major purchase.

But if a lot of these things were used it was necessary to record their exact location, and the specific radio frequency that each fake plant would emit. The slightest sloppiness or inexactitude meant that the artillery might send out a rain of shells and hit an allied unit, or our own troops, or civilians just out there where nobody was, or some deer. In addition, it was overlooked that the Vietnamese people, in general, do not perspire very much. Thoughtless of them to be sure. If the perspiration sensors were activated it more probably meant that an American unit was detected, something we should have known anyway.

The plastic plants, at least the ones I saw, did not look very much like other Southeast Asian flora; in fact they looked more like stylized hedges decorating Broadway stages. Other radio transmitter/perspiration detectors were used, some that mimicked piles of animal turds, even less convincingly. The records of these detectors became so hopelessly muddled that the information they provided was almost entirely ignored. We tried to turn these valuable technological marvels over to the Vietnamese.

At one point the captain of my ordnance support detachment was called home, and I was left in charge. I knew nothing about being a commander. The captain had given me good parting advice. He said let the sergeants take care of everything. Say nothing. Walk around as if you know what you're doing and never smile at anyone. The enlisted men will assume you are omniscient and leave you alone. I promised to heed that advice, even though I am a poor actor. And just as he was leaving for home he remembered a valuable gift.

The gift was three special connection links for fuel pumps. They were valuable. (You might pay attention here.) When there was a contact with the enemy and all hell was breaking loose, an actual firefight going on, helicopter gunships were called to the site. These helicopters, Hueys and Cobras, had machine guns in front and rocket pods on each side. Their arrival sometimes made the enemy disappear, run back into the jungle or duck into their tunnels. But not always. At times running away wasn't possible, and the enemy had to stand and fight. These firefights were awful and they could go on for some time with casualties mounting, medics on the ground calling desperately for evacuation flights. It's hard to forget the odd and curious sound of bullets zipping through the thick foliage. I remember trying to help bandage a man's shoulder and neck while someone was still firing at us. I remember how heavy he was when we tried to move him.

Helicopters use a great deal of fuel flying back and forth to a contact site and to medical stations or hospitals. They land and must be refueled as quickly as possible. The jet fuel they used, JP 4, essentially kerosene, was stored in large rubber bladders of thousands of gallons that lay, like beached whales, on the ground. The fuel had to be pumped quickly to the helicopter's tanks. A 350-gallon-per-minute trailer-mounted pump, powered by a small gasoline engine, was very essential for refueling. And the most essential part of the pump was the rubber-cushioned connection between the gasoline engine and the pump itself. And this most essential part of the most essential operation was in short supply. My departing captain handed me three of these valuable gizmos.

Anyone with a sense of military obligation would have put these three essential links back into service. After all, lives might depend on the rapid refueling of medevac helicopters. Two questions arose. First, why were these important little things in short supply? No one knew. They just were. They were requisitioned over and over but rarely showed up. They grew in trading value. One unit of a 350-gallon-per-minute fuel pump engine linkage was worth several boxes of frozen steaks, or several bottles of liquor, or a goodly amount of Cambodian hash. Obviously this rough black market was against army regulations, or should have been if anyone thought of it. But the real culprit was the supply system that failed to recognize repeated requisitions as evidence of need.

A second question was, what would happen to these valuable items if, prompted by one's conscience (my conscience in this case), they were turned in to the regular supply chain. Where would they go? Would they go to their intended role, possibly saving lives? Or would they simply return to the underground trading system used by persons without sufficient conscience? Obviously (and you will notice that the word *obviously* is used more and more often) they would be drawn out of the regular supply system by someone and traded for steaks or hash. These two questions rattled around in my head, and for a time I forgot all about the morality involved. And in a few weeks my tenure as interim commander of the detachment came happily to an end.

Which was a blessing. I did not like being in charge of the detachment or being in charge of anything for that matter. Some people enjoy command for the feeling of importance and power it produces. Some like to be commanded, to salute and march off with orders. I don't like either situation, nor do I like any people who like either situation. It would seem that in the army the act of command was simple. Every situation and its solution was addressed in the army regulations. Except that they weren't. It was thought to be so, but this assumption — that all eventualities had been thought of — was in itself a disaster. In addition, the management-by-following-the-rules approach might have worked in other armies, but not as well with Americans. Nothing works with Americans. They (well . . . we) don't follow orders very well. That underlying trait, coupled with the fact that in Vietnam most of the troops were there under duress, requires a stronger form of threat. What was the army going to do with disobeyers? Send them to Vietnam? My recollection is that troops were more or less tractable for about two weeks, and then they realized that obedience was little more than an option.

My detachment relocated from a large poorly secured area near Tay Ninh, near the Cambodian border, south to Bien Hoa, an endless sprawl of Asian wartime overpopulation near Saigon. We trucked all our tools and equipment down the road, fifty miles of dirt road, at ten miles an hour, raising clouds of dust in every village, running over innumerable chickens and dogs, and losing even more of the hearts and minds necessary to keep the support of the people. Our area in Bien Hoa was without water or regular electricity so we lived in tents, with a water truck and generators that ran all night. Everything we needed had to be built or produced by ourselves. Nearby another unit had several buildings, one-story structures that they weren't using. I tried to find out how we could take these over, but I couldn't find anyone with anything resembling authority. One night several of the armorers got up on top of the buildings with their rifles, and some beer, and announced that they had captured the buildings for our detachment. I deferred to the first sergeant as usual, and he thought the invasion was a fine idea. Still, I worried that if this turned out to be some sort of illegal move then I, as the officer in charge, would be blamed. In all the confusion no one seemed to notice. On other nights other men of our unit, seeing that you could get what you wanted by getting up on the roof with weapons, got up on the roof with weapons and announced various demands. The first sergeant said that they could stay up on the roof as long as they wanted.

Then, one day, while I was trying to figure out how to have my troops properly mix sulfuric acid for truck batteries, I was called to the battalion command headquarters. The acid had been shipped to us in five-gallon glass carboys at nearly 100 percent strength. It was extraordinarily dangerous stuff that could eat through uniforms, boots, and human skin instantaneously. The question was how much water to add to reduce the specific gravity to the right mix to be put in the dry batteries. The immediate question was whether to add the acid to the water or the water to the acid. There were no instructions present, but luckily one of the troops knew the right procedure, since I surely did not. I tore myself away from the battery acid operation and cleaned up a little and went to the headquarters.

The commanding officer, a reserve major, was guilty of taking the war, and himself, seriously. This was a dangerous sort of personality, prone to theatrically over-working the staff and giving patriotic talks to the men. He was probably at the most interesting and imaginative point in his life, full of military fustian, lots of saluting and squinting. He didn't like me, but by that time, about two months in country, I had lost my usual concern about personal popularity. On the desk in front of him was a letter from Senator George Aiken, my senator from Vermont to whom I had written, complaining about my misassignment. The major took a long minute to squint at me. But by this time I had been squinted at before, and this had almost no effect. I had heard that the army took a dim view of politicians interfering in their methods. And it was more than understandable that they should resist any senator or congressman trying to influence their operations or personnel assignments. The major inquired in clipped tones if I thought he had nothing to do all day but respond to politicians back home, prompted by complaints from miserable little shits like the one standing in front of him. He hadn't heard of George Aiken, or of Vermont, either, I thought. Senator Aiken, a venerable Republican of pronounced Yankee ethics, had famously condensed the frustration of the nation with the length and expense of the war by suggesting a terse solution. He said we should simply announce that we had won and come home. This solution had nearly universal appeal by being practical, pragmatic, and just slightly smart-assed. It was one of those suggestions that is probably impossible, but no one can tell you why.

Within days I was relieved of my temporary command and sent north to the division headquarters. I was given a brief welcoming interview with the commanding general. No one had the slightest idea what to do with me. The general asked if I understood Vietnamese. I admitted that at one point I did, but some time had passed, and a lot had been forgotten. That's just fine the general said tiredly. I'll do the best I can, I volunteered. Well, if you need anything . . . the general said, and turned to other concerns. I was left with the division chaplain for advice and guidance.

The chaplains in the Vietnam War, at least in the army, were oddly interesting. This chaplain became a friend. He was nominally a Catholic, intelligent and genial. I should have written down his name, and maybe his order. I should have written down a lot of things, but I didn't. We discussed the war and its deeper meanings, and he seemed to be a philosopher edging toward the secular side of religion. Even so he liked to examine our curious situation, in a war we both hated, but which we were pursuing against odds stacked against us, at least on a personal level. Being a war chaplain gave him points in his church career, a fact that he quietly confessed to be proud of. He counseled American troops of all faiths, and some ARVN soldiers, both Catholic and Buddhist. I asked him if being there and adding to America's impending defeat was the right thing for a thinking Christian to do. We agreed that to make the war turn out as the US government seemed to want would take a miracle. I had no interest in what made the Catholic Church run, but he told me that if nothing else they fed a lot of people who wouldn't be fed otherwise. He said it would help if I believed in God or miracles. I said I didn't believe in God. He asked well, then, how about in miracles? For example, he was also sure that there was no God. And that, he said, leaning over the table in the officers' mess (he had pale blue eyes and a map-of-Ireland face), that was the miracle.

10

You will remember that I began writing all this after a discussion about the war with a group of young people who had asked about it. I tried to make my role, if not heroic, at least understandable. Tales of all these failures of planning and operations, many years after the fact, illustrate that I also was personally a profound failure. It is the soldier's right to complain. The process of complaining should involve checking to see if your complaints were heeded and the faults corrected. But I never did, and that is shameful. Part of my self-excuse was that it was not my job to fix obvious shortfalls in planning. I wanted nothing from the army, or the war, but to get home safely.

The headquarters of the 1st Cavalry Division was in a town named Phuoc Vinh, the district capital of Binh Duong province. I have been back there, in 1993. There is nothing left of the American base. There is however a large golf course and club for Japanese businessmen. In 1969 the 1st Cavalry had taken over the base from units of the 1st Infantry and had expanded its area. The 1st Cavalry had also expanded its name to the 1st Air Cavalry with the inclusion of a great many helicopters. They had Hueys, the basic transportation helicopters; Loaches or light observation helicopters; and Cobras, narrow-bodied attack gunships, loaded with machine guns and rocket

pods. The tactical theory behind all these helicopters was that the army could move troops in, support their advance with rockets and machine-gun fire, and then pull the troops back out quickly after the effect had been gained. The only question not sufficiently answered was why. Why move into an area, shoot it up, and then retreat? No answer. But this was done time and time again. In short, it was part of a holding plan, holding until someone came forward with a long-range political solution. And as of 1969, no one had.

Helicopters filled the air, buzzing around, attacking the enemy, picking up wounded, dropping supplies to the troops in the field, delivering the mail, and taking certain troops to Saigon for an R&R week (rest and recuperation) or back to Tan Son Nhat when their yearlong assignment in Vietnam was over. Troops at E5 rank and below went by truck. It had seemed for the early years of the war that with enough helicopters you could control the military situation because you could move quickly, wait overhead until you saw something to shoot at, shoot at it, and then zip back to the security of your base. General Westmoreland was quoted saying that the army was "freed forever from the tyranny of terrain." This claim, boosted by its dim-witted alliteration, and probably not original with Westmoreland, hinted at a breakthrough in infantry tactics, solving most of the problems field commanders faced. Of course, there was a problem.

The problem was that helicopters were up in the air, above the fighting, not only visible for miles but also audible with a distinctive chopping sound. Besides, the Vietcong and the North Vietnamese had no helicopters, so that if the noise were heard it meant there were Americans, so shoot at them. And a second besides — helicopters are powered by turbines. Turbine engines' rear ends were red-hot exhaust orifices. The Russians had developed rudimentary heat-seeking missiles to use against jet fighters. These were too slow to catch American F-4s or other supersonic fighters. But they could easily detect a Huey helicopter, lumbering along through the air at three thousand feet, and fly up the turbine's exhaust pipe. The horrible prospect of having a surface-to-air missile fly up your exhaust pipe and blow you out of the sky made many pilots and commanders think again about what wonderful things helicopters were.

Phuoc Vinh base housed about three thousand US troops, trucks, commando cars, jeeps, helicopters, small fixed-wing aircraft, tents, bunkers, mess halls, command centers, communication centers, radio towers, water purification trailers, artillery batteries, large generators, storage trailers, impromptu showers, and outhouses. It had been built up over the years of the war without a real plan. Drainage hadn't been thought of, so that when it rained water collected in large ponds mixed with diesel fuel, garbage juice, and unclassifiable sewage. It most closely resembled an open sore on the earth in which people lived. The idea that the war might be a permanent thing evolved slowly. This idea directed that little thought be given to permanent structures. The Corps of Engineers kept the roads on the base more or less together by soaking them with a tar-based liquid. This stuff, called peneprime, was tracked everywhere, and made everything stick to everything else.

A second reference to Joseph Conrad if you'll permit. Joseph Conrad wrote that his main objective duty as a writer was "to make you hear, to make you feel . . . above all to make you see." I think you should also be asked to smell. The cool morning air at Phuoc Vinh base was mixed with a miasma of burning shit. The army had no choice but to incinerate its feces. Outhouses had no holes beneath them. Instead, fifty-five-gallon drums, cut down to about sixteen inches, were under each seat. In the mornings these pots were drawn out, filled with two inches of diesel fuel and a piece of cloth, and set afire. In time the whole mess burned off in thick, black clouds. It didn't do well to think about what you were breathing on a US Army base. There were supposedly humorous stories about the burn pots being placed back in under the seats while still smoldering and toasting some colonel's balls.

I was assigned to the intelligence people at the headquarters, again because I was supposedly a translator. I would help with interrogations and the seeking of information from prisoners of war, or civilians who might know something. At times these interrogations happened out in the jungle on a patrol with the infantry. So my plans to make all sorts of efforts to stay away from the infantry had failed. They failed not only because I wound up with the infantry anyway, but secondarily because nothing of any real value was gained from my interrogations. Not ever. Well, at least not intentionally or according to any plan. Sometimes we found out glaring shortfalls in parts of our own intelligence.

For example, on the base was a large trailer housing some computer equipment. The machines were made by the National Cash Register Company in an early attempt to welcome in the computer era. The machine operated on cards punched with an early form of code that is now so far back in computer memory as to raise a laugh among retirees at Microsoft. Nevertheless, the thing did sort of work. It swallowed thousands of cardboard cards and held the information on large spools of magnetic tape. It made loud noises and used a lot of electricity, both advantages in American military thinking. But for me, and others who wanted to be in the trailer with the NCR computer machines, there was another benefit. The computer and the cards had to be air-conditioned. Outside the trailer a generator and an air-conditioning unit hammered away, tended by a small Vietnamese man who sat under his very own lightbulb all night.

Americans raised to think that air-conditioning is specified in the Bill of Rights are always shocked and saddened in areas where it doesn't exist. If you were hot and sweaty in a place like Phuoc Vinh, and grimy with the dark morning air, climbing into an air-conditioned enclave was past wonderful. Silently you resolve that you will never leave, and if that can't be arranged, that you will come back as much as possible. Which I did. I spent time in the air-conditioned NCR trailer in my early weeks at Phuoc Vinh until I thought someone might notice I was missing.

But while hanging around the computer trailer and ardently thinking of passable reasons for me to remain there, I made another troubling discovery. The Vietnamese language, as I discussed tiresomely some pages back, is a tonal language. Each word has a diacritical tone mark accompanying it. There are six tones. There are also a number of added vowels and consonants shown with extra flourishes, dots and squiggles, on the basic phonetic alphabet characters. (I could show you, but it wouldn't help.) The designers and inventors at the National Cash Register Company did not include any of these diacritical marks or extra consonants in their machine, or in the printers that were attached. It didn't occur to them that Asian languages would be used in their printouts. (Communism had blinded people to the thought that Asians would ever have anything to do with computers.) As a result the printouts were as close to meaningless as they could be. Lists of the villages in Vietnam that were considered pacified, or pro-government, were produced, but without the extra little tone marks and unique consonants they had no meaning at all. And any attempt to decipher which place-names or village names or river names or road names were considered safe or passable, and which should be avoided or attacked, was not only useless but also possibly dangerous. These lists were distributed to unit commanders. The only saving feature might have been that the lists, if captured, were useless to the enemy as well.

I discussed this with the two specialists who manned the computer who, with no knowledge of or interest in the language, could barely fathom what the problem was. I explained to them that their work was worthless, and possibly misleading, even dangerously misleading, to any commanders creating infantry mission plans. To fix this was impossible of course, and there was a worse possibility. Horrible really, which you would understand only if you were there. If the computer work was declared useless someone might shut the whole thing down and the air-conditioning would be turned off. We spent time thinking about what to do.

I could see that my responsibility was to inform the highest level of the division command, the general or his staff, and warn that any reliance on these computer print-outs was dangerous. This required some talking to God, as it was called back then. But I finally succumbed to the advisability of doing the right thing. I made my doubts about useless computer-generated lists of intelligence known to one of the assistant division commanders, a one-star general. I showed him the useless printed lists of safe villages and pro-government areas. "What is that?" he asked. As I explained further I became slowly aware that he didn't even know about the computer, or anything about the language, or about tonal diacritical marks, or about the National Cash Register Company. But I had done my duty, and for the time being the air-conditioned computer trailer was safe.

What other actions could I have taken? Writing letters of complaint to authorities back home had to be thought through completely. Vietnam soldiers and veterans were suspect. The war was not just unpopular, it was loathed. That it was expensive and bloody paled next to the emerging realization that there was no end in sight. Lyndon Johnson said he could see the light at the end of the tunnel. This phrase, borrowed from politicians and generals seeking to quell dissatisfaction, sounded like desperate assurance and quickly became a laugh line. How did the US get into this tunnel in the first place, and why? What was the light? Promises of victory were scoffed at. The painful realization dawned that the Cold War was endless and pretty much meaningless and unwinnable, and certainly no longer cold. The idea of victory was tarnished and then laughed at. Vietnam was the hot part of the Cold War.

So my thoughts of writing a letter to someone up the line, or the government in Washington, or another whining complaint to George Aiken, remained on hold. The promise of a computer helping to win the war probably entertained military thinkers back in the US. But the thing didn't work. And in fact, it couldn't work. Forced to reveal their thinking, the Pentagon would have to admit that they had no idea what computers could do, or couldn't do, and that, in typical Pentagon style, they just bought a bunch of expensive things and wanted to see what would happen.

11

The war was a civil war in which the nation of Vietnam, divided north and south, was at war with itself. One side was communist and the other side, our side, was not. According to the political advisers the war resembled the misery of our own civil war, as well as other civil wars: the troubles between the north and south in Ireland, in Korea, the religious bloodletting in India, and so on. We were going to stay and win the hearts and minds of the South Vietnamese, and they would take over the fighting with conviction. Winning Hearts and Minds created a telltale acronym — WHAM — but that was just unfortunate.

How would the local population support the war effort? Several ways were suggested, all of them more theatrical than strategic. Of course, the South Vietnamese could send their sons off to join the ARVN, but what about the women with children, and people too young or too old to be part of an actual army? How could some citizens be organized to defend their own villages and farms? For this role some highly placed military thinkers, in the US and in South Vietnam, invented something called the DIOCC, the District Intelligence and Operations Control Center. You can tell by this long and glorious name that the idea was clumsy and ripe for failure. You can picture this on some oddball flow chart, a

PowerPoint slide, showing how local support would counter Vietcong activities. And assigned to this tactical nonsense near the Phuoc Vinh base was my friend Jack Desmond. Well, he was my friend for a while, but later he was not.

Small units of semi-military village forces were called regional forces and popular forces, or rough puffs. They were given guns and radios and someplace to gather. And they were assigned an American adviser. If they were lucky the adviser had a realistic opinion of how useless these efforts were and kept them out of harm's way. If they were less lucky they had someone like Jack Desmond. Jack was from the Boston area, and at first I thought I detected a suspicion in him that the war was a morbid joke and we should refrain from making it any worse. But as sometimes happens in war there is a hallucinogenic effect that makes men want to do something, anything, however ill advised. Something happened to Jack, and he got serious. He began to train his unit of mothers and grandparents, teenagers and walking wounded, to be able to mount operations, go on patrols, stand guard, and generally get in the way. He made plans pretty much all by himself.

I was, for a time, put on night operations duty. I was to make sure that our artillery wasn't fired at our own people or in areas where we might hit our own aircraft. I worked in a fortified bunker full of radios and maps. Flight plans and unit locations were all logged with us to avoid friendly-fire disasters. Jack did not log any such information with us. He had by that time only a moderate contact with reality. One day I spied Jack leading a troop of villagers off on a trail across some tapioca fields. They were armed, sort of, with rifles and a radio. On my own volition I went after this motley crew and caught up with them. Jack and I discussed what I saw as his tactical errors. His people were dressed in black pajamas and conical hats, pretty much the same outfit the Vietcong wore. They were accompanied by no helicopter support. There was no way of preventing their getting hit by our own artillery or shot by American troops. I asked him politely what the fucking hell he thought he was doing, and things went downhill from there. The members of his patrol watched us arguing and began to drift away. The concept of Americans as loons was not challenged that day.

No recognizable provision had ever been made for a person like Jack running his own operations even though what he did was in the best spirit of self-defense. The local villagers should have had the means to defend their own homes, but not on an ad hoc, disconnected basis, run by someone like Jack, who was, by that time, in a war movie starring himself.

I thought a bit and then wrote up a short report saying that Jack had gone off the rails and should be relieved. For a month or two, until he actually was recalled to his advisory headquarters in Saigon, he was at large in the Phuoc Vinh metropolitan area. I feared his anger at me personally might cost me something, and I was even more watchful than usual. Then he left, and I never saw him again.

The underlying fault was in the way the American effort was set up, which was not to fight civil wars. The American army command was arranged more or less on the design of the German General Staff with a bit of the French army thrown in, good God. There were four basic tasks: command, intelligence, operations, and supply. The second in the list, intelligence, was named the G-2 or the S-2, or in French the Deuxième Bureau. Or in Vietnamese Phong Hai, literally "the second room." I was becoming more valuable to the 1st Cavalry S-2 because, through no enthusiastic effort of my own, I was regaining my Vietnamese vocabulary. I could even understand conversations with some of the older farmers. Older Vietnamese in the countryside spoke their own concoctions of the language in which the tones, higher and lower, modulated and variegated, were strung together on a steady moan. It sounds like the underlying moan of a bagpipe.

I lived again with the hopelessly corrupt 9th ARVN during which time my fears for the end were strengthened. The 9th was more or less welcoming, but it wasn't sure about me. The ARVN had their families along. The American upper command hadn't thought about this.

Our generals put on a show of being tough-minded and dismissive of anything that looked like careful consideration and analysis, especially if it originated in younger, non-infantry officers. They hadn't known that ARVN bases included wives, grandparents, and children. Outside the limits of their bases, the ARVN families set up transient villages. ARVN soldiers got time off in between patrols to help construct an odd style of housing for their families, out of wood and steel planking. They were given sheet metal that had been printed with the labels of American beers. Back in the States, aluminum cans had taken over the market, and tons of surplus pre-printed steel beer can material showed up in the war zone.

Only some time later did I think that having your base surrounded by families, who were forced to live in makeshift villages, with babies being born, and children crying, and relatives mourning the daily toll of dead, was a form of defense. This was a civil war, fought to gain the support of the populace, winning their hearts and minds. North Vietnamese soldiers hated the ARVN, but not the innocent and suffering women and children with no place else to live. Maoist thought protected the people, and one didn't shoot them if it could be helped. In addition, just about every South Vietnamese soldier was experiencing a declining dedication to the South Vietnamese government with its corruption and self-preservation. If they lost a wife or a child in the fighting, they were more likely to blame the Americans or the avaricious officials in Saigon than the communists. The next war I am in I will not permit any allies to have their families build villages around the combat bases. I could not shake the comparison between my own baby son back home in Denver and the plight of the Vietnamese children living almost totally unprotected in shacks made of beer can metal.

The ARVN gave me an ARVN uniform, with my rank and name sewn on. It was, of course, the largest size they had, but still too small. I couldn't get into any of it, except the hat, also very snug. Luckily, I didn't have to explain why I wouldn't have put it on under any circumstances. In a box in a closet somewhere, I still have it. And the hat.

What I had learned, almost immediately living with the ARVN, was the difficulty, maybe the impossibility, of an alliance in a war. The South Vietnamese did not want to fight. They didn't value democracy very much. They didn't care whether they got to vote for their leaders. Their government had been so distant and criminal for so long that it might as well have not existed. So all the guns and vehicles and stuff we turned over to the ARVN were not immediately put to military use. Much of it was left in the weather, unassigned to any of the smaller units. Nor was the underlying reason for all these gifts a secret. The US was leaving as soon as it found a rationale. In 1969 the mood was desperation. And the ARVN were prescient in their lack of enthusiasm. The war would go on for five more years. Then the North would invade, and the remaining ARVN troops would take off their uniforms and run for it. It was said that Nixon and secret agent Kissinger were doing what they could to prolong the war so that Nixon would not be the first president to lose a war. Not a great reason to lay down your life. The final American situation would be as close to defeat as makes no difference. The only Americans who cared that Nixon and Kissinger would get blamed for the defeat were Nixon and Kissinger.

The assignments using my improving language skills were interesting but increasingly chancy. I nervously concluded that as the combat situation grew more confused and directionless, ideas about where to send Lieutenant Danziger, or Lieutenant Dangerous as he was mispronouncedly known to the ARVN liaisons, had less to do with logic and more to do with the flailing hope that new things should be tried simply because something had to be tried. Most attempts had failed. Support for the war at home had disappeared. Pentagon spokesmen had always given off the air of confidence and a can-do spirit. That was gone. A late decision was made to get rid of General Westmoreland, the man and the public relations disaster, and replace him with Creighton Abrams. Abrams was a tanker and thus a shorter man, compact and taciturn. I met him once, and for what it's worth I liked him. But Abrams took command of the army in Vietnam with the assignment to get out with something resembling that strange concept — honor. Nobody knew exactly what it

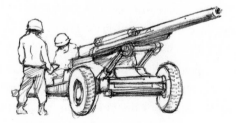

meant, and more probably no one cared so long as it ended. We first began to hear the Einstein definition of insanity.

As I said, the overall plan was to Vietnamize the war. We would build up the Army of the Republic of Vietnam, the ARVN, and then they would be responsible for the defense of South Vietnam, and democracy, and capitalism, and so on, and so forth. Then we could leave, announcing Peace with Honor. The lowest infantry rank could see that this dishonest stringing together of abstractions — peace and honor — was not going to work. Death with honor maybe, but any attempt to leave things to the South Vietnamese would be a disaster. The plan was mainly devised to shift the blame. It was a plan unequaled in misery, cowardice, and cruelty. A few diplomats objected but they were shouted down.

To fully appreciate the waste of war you had to visit an area near Saigon called Long Binh. Long Binh had grown rapidly with the war from a series of rice fields to an open scar on the earth where all the American detritus was left. There was some order to this dump. Things were put in piles labeled and fenced. By the end of the 1960s the fences had collapsed and the mountain of unusable artillery tubes bled into the mountain of junked helicopters. Children scrambled through this hellish range of piles, sent there to collect anything of removable value. The wrecked helicopters had been brought by other helicopters and dropped. A helicopter mountain grew to probably a hundred feet high. It was unstable as well. One item that had souvenir value was the clock from the Hueys. These could be, with skill and perseverance, removed and sold

to GIs for about ten dollars. From time to time the unstable mountain of helicopters would shift and some little Vietnamese kids would be trapped in the mass.

Other areas of interest at Long Binh included an area called axle valley. The bodies of old trucks, deuce and a halfs, either worn out or blown up were left there with no value except their wheel bearings. In the army scheme of supply, bearings were to be salvaged and used to keep other trucks on the road. Consequently, bearings were not in the supply chain. New bearings cost very little so the savings here were completely fictitious, and thoroughly ineffective, except as they further convinced everyone that idiots were running things.

The idiots also required that vehicles lost in combat had to be accounted for. Missing vehicles could be charged against unit commanders, who presumably had other things to worry about. Vehicles from the largest tractor trailer down to the compact motorized four-wheel platforms known as mules all had to be accounted for. Each had a plate riveted inside with a serial number. These plates were all removed and stored in some safe place so that any vehicle missing could be safely reported as a combat loss.

Obviously, I am going on and on about these incidents of military stupidity much too long. You have my apologies. (You could skip ahead to the end, but it just gets worse.) The details tell the progress of my own descent into the maelstrom of hopelessness. You simply could not think of the war as anything good or decent, as anything intelligent or logical, as anything that any sane person could defend. If you were raised to think of the past American war efforts as containing at least a portion of salvation, of being labors against evil, of being attractive to honest-if-simple men who were called forth, then all that was reversed by the sight of the waste and detritus of American war garbage.

Long Binh was also the site of an army jail, cells made of steel shipping boxes. Here Americans who had been court-martialed, or who were remanded for other reasons, were kept. It wasn't pleasant. The steel boxes were shipping containers, hot in the tropical heat, so miserable that if prisoners weren't mad going in they were when they came out. Long Binh Jail, abbreviated "LBJ" appropriately, was investigated by some journalists who had a hard time finding words.

Trucks arrived daily at Long Binh, dumping the war junk, and trucks left daily, taking scrap steel and other resalable material off to the markets of Saigon. One of the largest market areas was called Cho Lon, which literally means "big market." It was almost exclusively Chinese. It was here in this brawling, crowded intricacy of Chinese men, women, and children, scratching through old batteries for the lead plates, pulling apart telephones for the copper, cutting smaller panes of glass out of larger broken panes, pounding anything made of stainless steel, anything made of aluminum, anything made of copper into measurable lumps to be weighed. It was here that I first thought that the Chinese were better capitalists than anyone thought and that they had no love for communism. Tires were cut up into sandals, cut into strips and made into mats, into roofing tiles, into irrigation pipes, even into an odd form of jewelry. I made only one trip to Cho Lon, which was enough.

Part of the Vietnamization plan was a period in which the American forces continued to fight and keep the North Vietnamese from advancing into the South, at least not visibly, at least not before the Vietnamization plan shifted the blame to the ARVN. The fighting went on. The American deaths were reduced, but the American wounded grew. Only the decline in US deaths was made public, not the many wounded. When I was called back to the 1st Cavalry headquarters, I was asked what the ARVN troops thought of Vietnamization. I had learned by this time to mumble and look around, and then to disappear. It made no difference what I said because the ARVN condition was already fully known. The only American officers who really worried about the outcome of the war were the West Point graduates, for whom the army was a career. (West Point teaches history probably better than most universities.) West Pointers were, by that time, a gloomy group, comparing their lives to Wehrmacht officers in the last days of World War II, realizing that there was no way out, no salvation, and that if they were lucky, they would be alive, and barely that, at the end. And with any luck they could get a promotion and a few medals to impress people who were impressed by medals.

12

At the 1st Cavalry headquarters there were three generals. The main guy was a lieutenant general, a three-star, helped by two one-stars, brigadier generals. One of these brigadier generals, sensing that time was running out and that he should make whatever progress in rank he could as quickly as possible, decided to get himself a rather important medal — a Silver Star. The Silver Star means you have really done something, possibly heroic, possibly danger-ous. The verbiage is pretty specific, calling for places and dates and names. The brigadier, thinking he could operate unseen under the shroud of combat confusion, made up some exploit starring himself. At the headquarters one of the adjutant clerks had a book with the exact words needed for each medal, up to and including the Congressional Medal of Honor. Each medal specified the conditions of bravery or lack of fear, willingness to sacrifice, possibly beyond the call of duty. It specified further how far beyond the call: way beyond, a little bit beyond, right there at the precise amount of duty, and so on. The general, who prob-ably went into advertising after the war, wrote of an instance in which he was right there at the Silver Star level of perfor-mance. It turned out that, in the democratic American way of thinking, anyone could put anyone else in for a medal. Anyone — including himself. I wish I could tell the exact situation, but the whole enterprise blew up. The adjutant or someone was suborned in some way to enter the application. Then word got out to a journalist from *Time* magazine. The general disappeared in a cloud of ass saving.

I had access to this book of required descriptions for each level of medal and read it briefly. It fit into the *Catch*-22 mode of thinking growing in my mind. For non-army people such a book seems unnecessary, but the army tries to pre-think everything.

On Phuoc Vinh base, in the heat and the nightly mortars, there was a USO hut that provided coffee and donuts and other pastries sent by well-wishers back in the States. The coffee and donuts were served by very brave young women, recruited for the war zone for three-month stays. They were a welcome sight, lovely or not, and some of them were very pretty. They served the soldiers and made small talk. At the USO hut an enlisted man fell madly in love with one of the women and was driven mad by her presence. The woman was due to leave soon. The poor man would probably never see her again. He tried to express his love, but he could see that the whole thing was impossible. Besides, and this is important, she had been courted at the same time, if that's the right word, by an officer, a major, somewhat older and probably married with children. He worked in a sort of Quonset hut with sides open to the weather. One day the enlisted man, driven even madder by the unfairness and inequity of rank and the immediacy of his ardor, threw a grenade into the open side of the building, into the major's office.

But here was something the medal manual did not fully foresee. Fragging — that is, throwing a fragmentation grenade at an officer — was a frequent and rather serious means of expressing protest against commanders. Sometimes a gas grenade would be used. Tear gas didn't kill anyone, but it did make the protest known, and it lasted several days. Sometimes a claymore mine, which shot a wall of steel balls at the target, was placed pointed at the offending commander but not exploded. Just the sight of one was a sort of memento mori. In this case the lovelorn enlisted man had only wanted to scare the major. He did not remove the pin in the grenade. The thing came through the window, thudded on the floor, and before anyone could think, a heroic soldier in the office, who probably could not have seen that the pin remained, threw his body on the grenade to save the others. If the grenade had exploded, he would have been killed almost surely, or grievously wounded, and the reward for such a sacrificial lack of self-concern would have been the Congressional Medal of Honor, the highest award the United States provides. Reports of soldiers in foxholes who jumped on grenades to save their buddies in World War II were well known. It does seem an act of extraordinary sacrifice.

No suggested award descriptions seemed to cover the slightly less sacrificial situation in which the grenade does not explode. A judgment solely on the basis of mental heroism should result in the same medal rewarded, and gratitude from everyone. The division commander thought so, but as the report of this odd circumstance went up the line, asking for the highest medal, some exceptions were noted. Did the hero know that the pin was still there? If he didn't know, how do we know that he didn't know? And so on. In the end, the hero was awarded a Silver Star, impressive but not the highest level. If it had been me I think I would have felt cheated by events. But then, if it had been me, the question wouldn't have arisen at all.

13

You will read that by statistics 1968 was the deadliest year of the war. More Americans were killed during that year, as well as more South Vietnamese and more enemy. Some careless analysts will call 1968 the most dangerous year. But the years after 1968 were very dangerous in a different way, a way worth analyzing even this far beyond in time and in American policy. In short, from 1968 on the thinking about what to do entered a confused and almost hopeless state. It dawned slowly and painfully on American politicians and American voters that a victory was not only doubtful, but unidentifiable even if it did come along. Some concepts — victory, truth, love, wealth — reach a point where they are made manifest as either possible or impossible. Americans thought, or were made to think, that they had been victorious in the Second World War, but what was the real truth? Maybe it was victory and maybe it was something far less. The superiority of American forces was mostly a Hollywood version since Americans don't want to see movies in which the US loses. We want to be happy and to leave the theater happy.

In an emerging surprise it turned out that quitting the war, coming home, abandoning the effort, admitting mistakes, owning the disaster, and realizing that we couldn't inflict our will on a third-world nation — all that was not only difficult but provably not doable. In addition, what did a government or even the approving press say to explain that the large number of American war dead, and the even larger number of horribly wounded, had been sacrificed for essentially nothing, or at least no worthwhile gain? The really dangerous question that would rattle around for decades, and cost many people their careers, was: Who thought this was a good idea? The mistakes made by the US government and the military leaders at the Pentagon and the academies had been effected and propounded against obvious and solid counterarguments. Historians compared the brainless tactics of the generals in the First World War, ordering their troops forward against machine guns, to the steady increase of bombing, the escalation of troop levels, and the shameless lying about how things were going.

After 1968 half of the conflict was at home. The country was disgusted by the number of deaths, the horrible wounds, and the bottomless expense. And there were the social inequities asking which classes, economic and even geographic classes, did the fighting. (William F. Buckley pointed out that during the operative years of the war, 1965 to 1975, the Ivy League universities graduated in excess of twenty thousand men, of whom eleven were killed in Vietnam.) Not only were the Pentagon's assumptions wrong but also, it later turned out, the Pentagon knew they were wrong. This was kept secret. One bad idea followed another. The draft was a bad idea. The reliance on commandeered allies, Australia and Korea, was a bad idea. The reliance on massive aerial bombing attacks, dropping bombs into endless tracts of impenetrable jungle, was a bad idea. And of all bad ideas, the most incomplete and self-delusional thinking was the Pentagon's thinking about China.

A brief glance at a map shows that China was North Vietnam's immediate neighbor and main ally, supplier, and backup. It was the largest nation, the most populated, the most dictatorial, and the most resentful of Western invasion. It was quite close to North Vietnam's capital, Hanoi. China was never, repeat never, going to permit an invasion, certainly not an anti-communist invasion, or anything that might be construed as an invasion, to succeed. And if the US could in effect wind up fighting China, where would it all end? Should anyone have concluded that the Maoist government would allow an American victory against a country that bordered their own? Wasn't China the inventor of military maneuvers such as the human wave attack? And wasn't China's main problem overpopulation? Didn't Chairman Mao say that China's main problem was "too many Chinese"?

For a time after my period with the ARVN forces, and their wives and children, I was assigned to the 11th Armored Cavalry Regiment. *Armored cavalry* means the infantry rides in heavily shielded tracked vehicles, called M113s. Bullets will bounce off, but road mines will destroy the M113 and kill everyone inside. Men riding these things usually rode on top rather than inside, giving them a little more protection from mines, but none from anyone shooting at them. These were difficult decisions — inside or on top — and I didn't enjoy my time with the

11th ACR. They were brave men, but their assignments were stupidly dangerous.

Here was one of the worst of a list of bad ideas. At the ambassadorial level, a shameful agreement had been struck between the South Vietnamese government and the American advisers. It was a money deal. It was ordered that no artillery would be fired into rubber plantations. Rubber was one of the few cash crops that South Vietnam produced, and the plantations were amazing. Most were the property of the Michelin tire company. They were huge affairs, square miles of countless rows of tall rubber trees, perfectly straight, hundreds of thousands of trees with endless one-lane roads between them. The milky rubber sap was drained from chevron cuts in the trees by crews of ladies. They emptied the little collection cups every day into donkey-drawn tank carts, a labor of such mindless tedium that they welcomed the sight of the 11th ACR roaring by, waving and shouting at them. The collected rubber sap was heated and coagulated so the solid latex floated and was skimmed off. Part was smoked into a semi-translucent stretchy rubber, and part steamed into crepe rubber. The rubber was packed into wooden crates and had the word MICHELIN stenciled on the side. The management at the processing plant was French. They were welcoming enough, probably to the Vietcong as well as to us, and they always had a supply of beer and ice available for guests.

But because of the suicidal proscription against using artillery that the US had agreed to, the rubber plantations became the perfect place for the Vietcong and the North Vietnamese to hide. And they did. They also built tunnels and sleeping holes among the trees. The only way to fight them was to send in infantry, on foot or riding along with the 11th ACR.

Few of the troops I met riding on these wild and dangerous patrols knew who Michelin was, and it was a little late to try to teach my fellow soldiers anything about the shameful history of French Indochina and the tire industry. They did know that without the threat of artillery the enemy was much more bold and willing to come out into the open and shoot at us. The tracked M113s were junk but they were fast. An allowable tactic was the strategic retreat. But retreat to where? Farther back down the road, where additional enemy waited safely among the trees? Or where mines had been planted? Or was it better to stay and meet the attack by shooting back and running, here and there, on foot between the endless rows, dodging from tree to tree, without effective communication other than shouting, watching for pit traps and trip wires? There was little doubt in my mind that I was in a Smedley Butler situation and that I was risking my precious life for an industrial concern, a tire company, and not even an American tire company.

(Smedley Butler, it's important to know if you don't already, was a veteran of the Mexican Revolution and World War I and the most highly decorated marine in US history at the time of his death. But while he was still alive, he wrote a little book called *War Is a Racket* in which he decried the obvious profit motive behind military action more than twenty-five years before Eisenhower, on his way out of the White House, warned about the "military–industrial complex.")

The reason for my assignment to the 11th ACR was that the South Vietnamese government was going to have to control the rubber plantations if they were going to control their country when the US left. The M113s were unreliable vehicles, made by a large American company called FMC. (*FMC* stood for "Food Machinery Corporation," and the main product had always been industrial bread-making machinery among other useful items. This was funny depending on your definition of *bread*.) The M113s stalled in the midst of fighting at times, and their failures had to be figured into the tactics and strategies. They became unleavable fighting positions in the middle of the plantations until one side or the other ran out of ammunition. If we couldn't get the M113s out of the plantations we were ordered not to leave them for the enemy. They weren't easy to destroy, and the destruction took risky time exposed to the enemy. I don't remember how the actual fighting began or ended. I just fired at everything with everyone else. But I do remember one soldier, new in country, who, in the middle of all the firing, beshat himself. He kept on firing.

We took some ARVN people along with us on our patrols into the rubber. I could see that no confidence was gained by our tactics or by the unreliable M113s. I was there to say something convincing about how, when the Americans left, the South Vietnamese would be able to continue the fight. There was, of course, nothing to be said. The obvious fact was that most of the vehicles were worn and near the end of their useful or reliable lives.

I returned to the 1st Cavalry headquarters in Phuoc Vinh. The North Vietnamese had replenished their supply of mortars and rockets. Each evening they shot fifty or sixty mortar shells into the air, along with half a dozen 122 mm rockets. Unless you were in the clear and near the target of the 82 mm mortars there was not much chance of getting hit. The rockets were a different matter. The explosions were huge. They were of Chinese manufacture, clumsy and inaccurate. Sometimes they blew up early and killed the people who were preparing to fire them. Chinese weapons are much more reliable today. The North Vietnamese were now the main enemy for us, and they had increased in number and weaponry by 1969. The backing by the Chinese government had also increased.

Every night mortars fell out of the sky, usually in brackets of three. The 1st Cavalry commander was amazed at how destabilizing such a simple weapon could be. The mortar itself is little more than a tube and a base plate. There is a sighting device in the side, but someone with experience can be accurate just by eyesight reckoning. The targets are usually not killed, at least not by the 82 mm shells, but they are wounded. During the attack everyone dives under shelter. The greatest fear was that the enemy would cut through the wire and gain entrance to the base, running around, spreading terror and confusion, and setting satchel charges. An attack like that would be predicted by a long mortar barrage.

We answered mortar attacks with artillery. Hundreds of shells would race out into the lowering darkness in search of the mortars. But where were they? By this time in Vietnam, I was even more blood-sworn to my own preservation and determined not to do anything risky. I was assigned to something called a target acquisition squad, made up of me and three enlisted men. There was a theatrical portion to this staffing. You couldn't send out just enlisted men — that would look like you didn't value their lives as highly as the officers. So an officer had to be sent as well. Again, I realized that all my plans were failures, including my acceptance of a commission solely to gain more time stateside. Feeling like an even greater fool than before, I stayed with the target acquisition squad.

When mortars began to fall in the evening the target acquisition squad were ready to jump in a jeep and rush to the site of the first explosion. Mortars make craters, but these craters, unlike bomb craters, are not perfectly round. They are very slightly oval since the mortar shell comes in at an angle. In theory if you could find the longest diameter of the oval and plot it against the shortest diameter you could find the line of azimuth, in degrees, at which the mortar fell. Further, and this is theory as well, if you found the deepest part of the crater and compared it with the center of a crisscross made up of the shortest and longest diameters you could, with a plumb line, approximate the vertical angle of the falling mortar. Well, actually you could on a nice spring day in broad daylight, but not at night when other mortars were coming in. Besides, all this was based on the additional theory that mortars traveled in parabolic curves, meaning that the beginning of the arc was the same as its descent. Maybe they did on the nice spring day.

If we could find the first mortar crater, we set up a four-legged tripod, a quadrapod, and quickly oriented it to true north with the compass supplied on the top. All the numbers were then radioed back to the artillery batteries so they could, at least generally, start firing in a supposed direction. The greatest problem to finding a mortar attack source was that the calculation was, as I say, being done in the middle of a mortar attack. Further, this was being done by four people on the squad who didn't want to be there doing anything. To make up for the accurately evaluated inaccuracy of target-acquisition-squad-reported numbers, the artillery fired a large number of shells. A very large number of shells. The noise was deafening, but reassuring somehow. If you could hear it, it hadn't hit you.

I went on some crazed rides into the night. I don't think we reported any numbers or facts that added to the accuracy of the artillery. But we did have an accident. The driver of the jeep, who for some reason hadn't turned on the headlights, ran the jeep into a revetment, a short wall meant to shelter helicopters from shrapnel. The jeep turned over and we all, except the driver, were flung out. The driver and the other enlisted men were badly hurt, but I, using skills I didn't know I had, maybe left over from high school tumbling exercises, went into a some-what graceful roll and was unhurt. The others all received Purple Hearts, but I got nothing for my troubles.

Two incredibly bizarre assignments followed. The first is more difficult to explain because many Americans have forgotten who Bob Hope was. American humor at present is as vicious and destructive as any in the world, but in the 1950s and '60s, Americans were relatively gentle in their application of sarcasm and ridicule. Bob Hope was a comedian who was thought to be the last word in sophisticated smart-assitry. In actual practice he was pretty harmless. During World War II and the Korean War, Bob Hope was part of the entertainment provided for the troops. He seemed to make young soldiers feel that the folks back home were thinking of them and understood their sacrifices. His jokes were a little bit tough on the commanders, but not too much. His sarcasm was in an ain't-that-the-truth, nudging sort of way. He had some mild putdowns of American politicians and the president, but nothing deeper or anything that might hurt people in power. And he never, at least as far as I could tell, figured out, until it was too late, what was wrong in the Vietnam War. His job was to bolster esprit de corps, and in a way, I felt sorry for him. He could have shown some understanding of the stupidity and viciousness of the politicians and commanders who were running the war, but he didn't. A possible explanation was that he was preserving his own personal appeal for future use, or maybe he was too old or uncaring to side with the troops and tell the truth. In his later years he was repeat-

edly honored in Washington. I don't think he ever realized what being honored in Washington actually meant.

I was told to produce a roster of enlisted troops who
wanted to make a trip to a huge Bob Hope show in Saigon.
No one wanted to go to a huge Bob Hope show in Saigon.
I knew this would be difficult to explain so I made it a list
of persons who would go whether they wanted to or not.
There were benefits. A day off, a trip away from the stink
and mortars of Phuoc Vinh, and possibly some beer. And
a chance to ogle the dancing girls that Hope brought with
him — Raquel Welch and some other grinning pneu-
matic cretins. The show had always been a success on
aircraft carriers and at air force bases, but for the army,
hard against the shit and misery of the actual fighting, it
was simply awful. I went with my contingent to Saigon,
but I didn't go to the show itself. The army was treating
the soldiers as if they were dull, insensate brutes who
would be grateful if allowed to have a few jokes and see
some girls to drool over, and have a beer, and then go
back to the war. The army paid no attention to wise advisers who warned that Hope and his shows for the troops
were at best tolerated, and usually loathed.

I'll get to the second bizarre assignment presently, but I
want to mention that in all these assignments there was
nothing resembling a theme or a mission for an officer
who spoke the language of the people whom the US was
trying to help. No thought was given to what should be
done with Lieutenant Danziger to improve the chances of
victory. But that was not a special piece of neglect reserved
for Lieutenant Danziger. By 1969, George Aiken's advice

to say we won and leave was the only real possible way forward. Operations went on day after day: US troops were killed, maimed, blinded, and driven mad; Vietnamese soldiers and civilians were killed, maimed, blinded, and driven mad. Billions of dollars were wasted. Large parts of Vietnam were destroyed, plowed under, poisoned, and burned. The war was to last another five years, and all this without anything resembling a plan for victory, or even a plan for a plan. The army fought, the air force bombed, the navy . . . well, I don't know what the navy did.

I tried to avoid the worst of ideas, but since, as shown, I was a failure at most things, I was also a failure at avoiding the worst ideas. I have mentioned that the army is more or less structured on the German General Staff, with four basic staff divisions. To these was added a fifth group — civil affairs. In civil wars and in wars for the allegiance of the population, someone has to think up activities to help secure good relations with the people. Passing out food and medicine, building water systems and bridges, and generally being helpful around the house all contributed to gaining the respect if not the acquiescence of the bedraggled and shell-shocked citizens. But what activities could the army offer to rural people and at the same time keep itself aware and secure? Infantry officers wanted nothing to do with civil affairs. Some wanted to get going on the basic task of killing the enemy and ending the war. Some simply liked fighting. Civilians, even civilians who supported the American soldiers, were simply in the way. But killing civilians by accident is sure to produce bad publicity.

Even so the civilian administrations have standing in civil wars, and they can't simply be swept aside. Most difficult for many American commanders is the task of understanding other cultures. Some cultures are very strange. Asian cultures are the hardest and, for Americans, the strangest. At the very top of the American government, Lyndon Johnson tried manfully to understand what Ho Chi Minh wanted. He failed mostly because he failed to listen to anyone except the Pentagon, and all they listened to was one another. Every so often, however, the Vietnamese culture, with its strange religions, its history of battling the French and the Chinese, its brutal experience with the Japanese during World War II, and its underlying very tough stubborn gentleness, had to be countenanced. Added to all this were some absolutely bizarre superstitions. One such widely held belief was that of the Wandering Soul.

14

The Wandering Soul superstition held that if a Vietnamese person, a soldier for example, died, and the body was not returned to its proper burial ground to be in the company of dead family members, the soul might wander through the forests and the mountains forever. While wandering, and this is the shivering part, the soul might call out for help finding its way home, something you didn't want to hear in the dark. If you were hundreds of miles from your home in North Vietnam, with death a possibility from American bombs and artillery, and you were young and credulous, you might lose a lot of sleep if you heard a Wandering Soul moaning in supplication. You might go mad and refuse to fight further. You might go madder and influence your fellow soldiers to refuse to fight further. You might go completely off the rails and shoot yourself or your commanders. These dreadful possibilities all seemed like good ideas to the American commanders, so a plan was hatched, and I was involved in its execution. I thought the plan was crazy, but craziness was relative.

During the planning for this obvious insanity, other things occurred to challenge the Wandering Soul idea. One night a true tragedy unfolded, a night when I was assigned to be the officer of the day, or night, making a tour every hour of the green line around Phuoc Vinh base. The green line was a perimeter of decaying bunkers and unstable towers, all built for a war that was supposed to be over years ago. I was to examine weapons, check the communication lines and make sure they were operational, check to see that no booze or beer was present in the troops on guard, and generally represent authority.

I did the best I could. I went around in a jeep, stopping every so often, at random, walking into a bunker unannounced, acting as officerish as I could, looking for violations of the guard rules. There was supposed to be no marijuana, and nothing stronger. No one was supposed to be sleeping or even sitting resting with eyes closed. And there was to be no music, nothing that could hide the footfalls of the approaching enemy. There were about twenty-five bunkers and towers, each with a sector of the green line to cover. A no-man's-land of about thirty yards surrounded the base, lined with anti-personnel mines, claymore mines, trip flares, and barbed wire. The working condition of all this defensive matériel was my responsibility, at least for a twenty-four-hour space, and I was supposed to have checked it all.

Needless to say, I had checked nothing, not because I was shirking the work involved, but because checking mines and other explosives was dangerous. The officer of the day before, and of the day before that, felt the same trepidation. The wires and flares may not have been checked at all since their installation however long ago. No one seemed to know. I did check the floodlights, which weren't dangerous. The greatest fear in the night was that enemy sappers would breach the green line

bearing satchel charges. They would run around in the confusion, throwing these charges here and there, destroying helicopters, igniting fuel bladders, and setting off secondary explosions in the artillery ammunition storage. This had happened or was rumored to have happened on other bases with hundreds of casualties. But this time was different.

About two hours after nightfall, someone set off a trip wire in the no-man's-land, claymore mines went off, and an eruption of gunfire in one section of the green line roared out into the dark. The floodlights came on. Soldiers triggered additional claymores, and all the troops fired wildly across the no-man's-land and into the forest. After a few minutes the firing died down. The officer in charge, me, raced to the sector where things had exploded, shortly joined by the base commander, who demanded to know what had happened. I didn't know.

The floodlights showed that the intruders were not enemy soldiers. They were a group of young women from

Phuoc Vinh village, very young actually, who had been given directions and a map of a safe route through the perimeter, where the trip wires and mines had been disconnected. But either the map was wrong or their pimp got it wrong, or they did. They had all been killed, cut to ribbons by all the firing. In the white glare they were small figures, dressed in black, scattered in a line leading back to the trees. It was an awful sight. The following morning, women from the village, half a mile from the base, were let in to retrieve the bodies. Some of the dead women were daughters or young mothers, not really prostitutes, just trying to make some money. The women from the village were carefully accompanied by US soldiers who knew how to disconnect the wires. The bodies were loaded into a truck and driven off somewhere. The wires were reconnected. By that time my stint as officer of the day was over, and I returned to the Wandering Soul project.

Public address sound systems were affixed to helicopters and recordings were made of what we thought, or at least I thought, might sound like the voices of the troubled Wandering Souls. My idea was generally based on radio shows I had listened to as a kid that scared the bejeezus out of me. It wasn't a very good idea, but there was nothing else to go by. The script, which again was my idea, and again not a very good idea, had a voice identifying itself as a dead Vietnamese from some town near Hanoi. For years he, or she, or it, was trying to get home to be with its family. We made several rehearsals to play this piece of insanity from a helicopter at night over the base itself. The wailing voice, actually a woman who worked in MACV headquarters in Saigon, went over and over in a keening speech of sorrow that lasted about two minutes. Several of the helicopter pilots refused to fly these odd missions, complaining that they were having nightmares about their own souls wandering, even though they couldn't really understand what the voice was saying. An additional idea came from one of the brigadiers, an idiot I thought, who proposed that we add a bit of one of Nixon's speeches, sort of like a commercial break, in which he assured listeners we sought no wider war. And now back to our program.

I don't remember how long we ran the Wandering Soul tape, but it wasn't long. The whole project was as ludicrous as anything in the history of anti-communism, but at that point in the war zone, life had taken on many aspects for which the overused term *surreal* could accurately be applied. Here was a helicopter, flying at night over a section of Southeast Asian jungle, equipped with loudspeakers and recordings purporting to be the voices of the spirits of the undead, howling and weeping about being lost and consequently being very sad about it, written with almost no knowledge of the details of Vietnamese superstitions by an unfortunate military intelligence officer whose heart wasn't in it, with the supposed purpose of scaring enemy soldiers into surrender or revolt. Actually, the word *surreal* is left far behind. And worse — we all knew that the project was inane, worthless, laughable, wasteful, and possibly dangerous, but we went ahead with it anyway. It hurts to think that all this was true.

Whether operation Wandering Soul frightened the enemy we had no way of knowing. But it did scare some of our allies. Some South Vietnamese units nearby were threatening mutiny. We hadn't thought of that. It was abandoned after that, and the tapes, my first attempt at theater, were hopefully destroyed.

The Vietnam War was at least on paper a civil war. The North, communist and backed by the Russians and the Chinese, fought to unify the country with the South, backed by the US and some allies. So if a Vietnamese citizen from north of the demilitarized zone, despite his early allegiance to Ho Chi Minh, woke up one morning and saw the error of his ways and desired to join the South Vietnamese side and fight for capitalism and democracy, he was permitted to do so, and, again at least on paper, welcomed. We dropped millions of safe-conduct passes over the jungle. The cartoons on the passes showed a before-and-after situation. The before was death and misery in the jungle under American bombardment, and the after was food, shelter, and friendly acceptance. It seemed to be an open-and-shut case. North Vietnamese soldiers could take these passes to any ARVN or US troop and be welcomed to a new life in democratic South Vietnam. They would be fed, medicated, given a place to sleep, and sent to a reeducation camp to get their minds right. If they were sick with malaria or wounded, they might be encouraged by their own commanders to surrender rather than be a drag on the efforts of the healthy. The initial interview, when one of these enlightened people came forward, was done by the military intelligence people. The program was called Chieu Hoi, which meant "open arms," or, in the unfunny humor of the times, "out of ammunition."

The majority of the surrendering people were women, often North Vietnamese army nurses who were either desperately malarial, or pregnant, or both. My commander at the 1st Cavalry had the idea that we could get valuable information from the women by promising them benefits for their unborn. Exactly where he got this idea was unclear, perhaps somewhere at his own mother's knee. But I was told to make promises, most of which were truthful. A few enemy babies were born in the 1st Cavalry MASH unit.

Some enemy troops surrendered when they were wounded. My commander further hypothesized that they should undergo any surgery without anesthesia. His idea was that they would cry out valuable tactical information. This was, of course, nonsense. I was detailed to be in the MASH unit when they were operated on. Since I couldn't understand the screams of North Vietnamese soldiers, I took an ARVN translator along with me. He couldn't understand anything, either. One poor unlucky young man had been hit with a claymore mine, which sprayed him with dozens of steel ball bearings. He never lost consciousness and screamed *Troi Oi!* — Oh, God! — over and over. The MASH surgeons, who thought they were immune to the screams of the suffering, dug out the ball bearings one at a time. Obviously, operating on a human being without anesthesia was something new to them. After about fifteen minutes of waiting to hear something of tactical value, other than screams, I told them to put him out. And they did. Of all the difficult-to-forget days in my war experience this was the worst. There was a lot of blood.

The work of the war ground on, day after day. Duties for officers were assigned on rosters. In this way the combination of upcoming side tasks, some dangerous, some trivial, could be planned for and possibly avoided by circuitous means. I tried to avoid the duty of having to account for stolen or missing property. It is surprising that property is so important in a war, but in the Vietnam War the army was never sure what the outcome was going to be. Vehicles, weapons, generators, and even cooking equipment had to be accounted for. A commander taking over a unit would be responsible for all the unit's properties, and he would want to be somewhat sure that it existed. If it was gone or destroyed there had to be some piece of paper.

This curious form was called a "report of survey," which meant that we had looked for it and here's what we saw. I was handed several assignments to account for stuff. A soldier in one Phuoc Vinh unit had gone crazy and driven off with a jeep, south to Saigon. He had been caught when he sold the jeep somewhere in the clogged warrens of Bien Hoa and was jailed for a few weeks. I was supposed to go down to Saigon and get him to sign something admitting the theft. Flying down to Saigon, to the replacement compound, we were fired on several times, which is unpleasant at best. And the jeep thief wasn't there anyway; he had already been shipped back to the States for punishment and discharge. The jeep wasn't retrieved. Whatever risk I had been forced to take to account for the jeep was totally unjustified, certainly in my mind. The report of survey closed with the choice of words "taken by person or persons unknown." A quick, non-dangerous look around, maybe ten minutes' worth, could have arrived at the same conclusion. I returned by truck, somewhat safer.

I also was periodically assigned to certify casualty reports. When a US soldier was killed and brought back from the field, his body was taken to an impromptu morgue called the graves registration unit. Reports of deaths to be sent to families had to be done as quickly as possible. Commanders had to write something about the bravery of the soldier and the pride of the nation and so on. But mistakes were often made, which were unforgivable and embarrassing, resulting in angry parents, distraught wives, and outraged congressmen. The army had reported sons and husbands killed who weren't. The worst part of checking was a required visit to the graves registration morgue. I was supposed to see the body, open the body bag, check the ID tag, and sign off that I had done so. The graves registration unit, with its odor of death, its pounding refrigeration trailers, and its cemetery mood, was possibly the most miserable duty in the entire army. The dead were nearly all young, and their deaths all unexplainable.

Daily life at Phuoc Vinh grew worse. I lived in a sort of bunker made of wooden boxes filled with sand. Around the base the engineers had built a wall of sandbags as well. The entire hunched structure was covered with green canvas tarpaulin held in place with more sandbags. For a while I was on a night duty, manning the radio and communicating with the helicopters that flew around looking for signs of enemy activity. We had to know where our helicopters were so the artillery didn't shoot them out of the sky. I had a bunk bed in my room, and for a while a slightly crazy American warrant officer pilot lived with me. Then he moved out and I had the room to myself for a few days. This was actually a rare luxury on Phuoc Vinh base.

Then a North Vietnamese artillery officer came to the gate of Phuoc Vinh base and surrendered. His name was Kuat Minh Ngoc. Our commander — who despite my snarky comments about him was actually one of the better full colonels I had met — wanted to keep Kuat Minh Ngoc at our base as long as possible. By the rules Kuat had to be turned over to the South Vietnamese army as a prisoner, not a pleasant prospect. He was extremely sick with malaria and probably would have died if he had stayed in the forests much longer. He decided that he wanted to surrender and live. He may have been sincere. He had been in the woods for two years, living in holes and ducking American artillery. We gave him quinine, some food, and soon he felt better physically and more at peace with his decision to switch sides. He seemed to be an extremely gentle person from a family of pineapple and tapioca farmers in the North. After three days, during which he lived in the top bunk in my room, we had to decide what to do with him. I began bringing his meals over to him and got no complaints about the food. We had gotten some information from him, some numbers about the supply of mortars and rockets that the colonel considered useful — actually none of what he told us was of any use — and he might have told us more, but he couldn't stay with us. He recuperated, sleeping in my room for about a week, talking to us every evening. My .45 automatic pistol hung in its holster on the wall during all this time, because it didn't occur to me to put it someplace safe. This was rather stupid of me, a safety lapse I mentioned to no one.

Reluctantly we turned him over to the South Vietnamese army, and he disappeared in a truck headed south for reeducation. I had grown to like him, and I was sorry to see him go. The colonel was surprised to hear that he was gone. After a day of thought he told me to investigate how we could get him back and make use of his knowledge of the enemy artillery strengths. The granting of such an exception to the rules could only come from the US embassy in Saigon, about fifty miles to the south. The rules on surrender had been strictly worked out between the US and the South Vietnam diplomats, and only they could make exceptions. This meant driving down to Saigon, finding the embassy, making the request, getting the approval, and then finding Kuat Minh Ngoc wherever he was getting reeducated. You would think there would have been some foresight or protocol about a situation like this, but there wasn't.

I took two enlisted troops with me in a jeep, one driving, one riding shotgun, with me and my interpreter in the backseat. I could have made the trip by helicopter, but I had resolved that unless absolutely necessary I would stay on the ground. But I didn't know where the embassy was, or how to find our way through the endless crowded shantytown outskirts of Saigon where the roads lost all definition. An Asian city in the middle of a war spends no effort making the approaches clear to the traveler. There were no maps. We drove around, up and down a selection of promising routes, blocked by sludgy canals and haphazard markets. I had made two mistakes. First, we were using up our gas, and second, it was Sunday. Sunday in the army was just another day since the war went on endlessly. But for the US embassy, following State Department rules, Sunday was a day of rest. So was Saturday. The embassy, even in the middle of all the fighting and confusion, stuck to a schedule of a proper ambassadorial workweek. So when we finally found the embassy compound, the very same place that would later become world famous for helicopters leaving the roof as the North Vietnamese army entered the city, the gates were locked. A young Filipino guard was on duty.

I had made a contact with a full colonel who was working, and who fortunately saw us from his window. He came down and told the Filipino guard to let us in. This took some time and a frustrating phone call from the guard to someone. The colonel seemed to have no requisite authority. The whole thing was becoming asinine. We, the colonel and I, looked completely idiotic in front of the enlisted men, something that was to be avoided if possible. The colonel took me up to his office and typed an impromptu letter to someone in the South Vietnamese government to allow us to take Kuat Minh Ngoc back to Phuoc Vinh for additional intelligence research. Or something. The letter struck me as completely unconvincing. I thanked him, and we got ready to leave. It was also interesting to see a full colonel typing.

In the compound of the embassy buildings there was a car pool and some gas pumps. We were nearly out of gas, and we tried to fill up. But the pumps were all locked for

the weekend. Another assiduous Filipino showed up and explained, excitedly, that we couldn't have any fuel because this was state department gas and could not be used in any military manner. It was his job to protect it. The idea that we were all on the same side didn't impress him. He wasn't impressed when I took out my aforementioned .45 pistol and waved it at him. Or when I pointed it at his head with loud instructions to unlock the pump. Looking out the window, the colonel/typist saw this contentious scene and came running down. My driver and shotgun man were aghast that an American colonel could not order a Filipino guard to unlock a gas pump to provide gas for an American army jeep. But the guard was obdurate. Scared to death with Americans waving weapons at him, but obdurate.

In the end the colonel and I siphoned gas out of two state department Fords, and we left. By that time it was late in the day, and any thought of retrieving Kuat Minh Ngoc from the South Vietnamese reeducation camp, or wherever he was, had faded into unimportance. We drove back north to Phuoc Vinh in sullen anger, made more painful in my case because I was made to look like more of a fool than I knew myself to be. I never saw Kuat Minh Ngoc again, and I vowed to have no more to do with the goddamn US Department of State or, for that matter, the entire Philippine nation.

15

In the years since the war, I have read a number of books about the military and the political reasons for the American efforts, the successes and failures. To conclude that the full ten years of the war were valueless is a mistake, but a traditional victory it was not. Even back in the States there was no parade, no celebration for many years. The Vietnam Veterans Memorial in Washington took decades to complete, and it is still unclear what it means, reflective sadness to some and an insult to others. Many soldiers, politicians, and journalists have tried to explain what happened and where things, at least for the United States, went wrong. Was the war effort a product of American pride, bombast, and stupidity, or was it absolutely prescient in its opposition to communism? The following years have shown clearly that the Vietnamese, North and South, and their border friends, the Chinese, at heart did not want to be communist. The Chinese were and are capitalists to the bone, to an even greater degree than the Americans who were ready to fight to tell them what they should be. They work hard and they like money. They like industry. They like getting rich. And as we see now, they are driven by an Asian version of international mercantilism, furiously driven to establish market colonies in parts of the world that once tried to colonize them.

The best nonfiction book on the war came out in 1988 by a former war journalist, Neil Sheehan. Titled *A Bright Shining Lie*, it told in hellish detail of endless American waste and failure. It told of intelligence ignored and wisdom cast aside. The book is too great an accomplishment to try to summarize here, and I would not attempt to do so without a complete rereading, but it is a majestic work that took Sheehan more than ten years to complete. It established him as the foremost authority on this sad period of American history, the blindness, the carelessness, the cruelty, and a particular American brand of dimness and illogic.

After he finished the book, Sheehan came around on a book tour, and I was detailed by my newspaper in Boston to interview him since I was the only veteran on their staff. He was unsmiling, dour, and seemed, when I talked with him, very tired. We sat for a time and talked about the army, the country, and some politicians who figure in the story. He had raked over the history and the lessons of the war so many times that much of his talk seemed to be rote — and sadly so, as if further explanation to someone like me was probably not going to accomplish much. But he was gentle and took as much time as I wanted. At the end of the interview I had come to like him very much and appreciated his obvious dedication to getting the story right, even if it had diminished his affection for mankind and his country, and taken many years of his life. But at the end of the interview I asked him what, in so many words, the war meant.

He paused and said, looking, not at me, but at the floor, "They'll never be able to do that again."

I am not sure exactly how I put my response, but I waited a moment and said something like well, Mr. Sheehan, you're a smarter man than I am, and you clearly know more than I ever will, but I think you're wrong.

They, whoever he meant by "they," could certainly do it again, and as the years have shown, they have tried to do it again. And again. Whatever the lessons of Vietnam were, they have been ignored and subsumed by administrations and congresses and courts. Thus, although I remember I didn't say it at the time, what Americans learned by the inglorious conclusion of the war was not that there are provable limits to military solutions. They learned that failure could be ignored. In fact, if there is any reason for what I am writing today, fifty-plus years on, it is that we seem doomed to a sort of Vietnam-like quagmire every few decades. I can only begin to feel what deepening sadness Neil Sheehan must have felt watching the endless scrub wars and secret bombing campaigns that have, at least in my opinion, proved him wrong. A friend said we are an optimistic people, and that's the problem. But there is another definition of optimism, sometimes called Jewish optimism, that says things are bad, but they could be worse.

In 1970 a good part of the army, the higher commands and the civilian authorities, were finally ready, as the decade rolled over, to face the truth of how hopeless things had gotten. The war, and the prosecution of it by the US, was ruining not the Vietnamese communists, but the American army. The civilian strife at home, with families and generations erupting in violent disharmony, with racial hatreds brought forward from wherever they

were hiding, and with the costs mounting astronomically — all that was bad enough. But the evidence that the army itself was emerging as a casualty could not be ignored.

A great deal of the United States' standing in the world, and in places a lot more important than the comparatively insignificant country of Vietnam, was based on the perceived strength of our military. If we had cut and run in 1970, as bad as that would look, we could have begun rebuilding both in reputation and reality. But if we stayed and continued this long, awful, destructive slog to what could only be defeat, our reputation, and the power it conferred, would be lost forever. How could a nation that had been a major factor in winning the Second World War lose to a third-rate former colonial nonentity like North Vietnam? Even if that question were never actually asked, the doubt and the perception of weakness would affect American success in much more important struggles. And worse, it would show that the United States, which thought it was unbeatable, was beatable.

What was needed was a way out, and that required a demonstration of power, a telling and provable win against the communists, an act to threaten and scare anyone else getting ideas about listening to Soviet promises. We had come to Vietnam to advise and train the South Vietnam forces, to support the government, and to make a stand for democratic capitalism. We had in fact failed in all three aims, but some sort of final victory, even if it only lasted for enough time, a year, a few months, whatever we could get, would allow a less ignominious retreat for the US.

16

The way out was called Lam Son 719, an operation named after a small village with historical significance to the Vietnamese. Lam Son was the birthplace of Le Loi, a legendary Vietnamese emperor who held back the Chinese attempts to subjugate the country way back in the 1400s. Amazingly Le Loi was able to do this without American advisers. Operation Lam Son would empower the South Vietnamese army, after years of training and even more years of being advised by the United States, push the North back across the Laotian border and into the hills, and cut off the Ho Chi Minh Trail. The trail by that time was nearly a mile wide, made up of myriad smaller trails and roads. It had been bombed ceaselessly so that it was jungle scar tissue, overgrown in places and barren in others. Arms and supplies were carried just as ceaselessly among the thousands of craters. The plan was for the Army of the Republic of Vietnam to enter Laos and cut off this valuable supply line. The operation went on despite the fact that no one, no American officer or ARVN officer, no American politician, no student of military history, and none of America's allies, had any confidence that it would work.

To help make matters infinitely worse, the United States Congress, torn by indecision and distrust, enacted a

restriction that no American soldiers were to accompany the ARVN. That sort of meant that no US soldiers could be in Cambodia or Laos. But the American command interpreted this restriction narrowly, taking it to mean that US personnel could not be on the ground but could still be in the air, piloting helicopters. Obviously, this was a clever way of disobeying the congressional intent, but no one seemed to be able to stop this horrible and frankly dishonest interpretation.

Coupled with the clumsiness and impossibility of these decisions was the reopening of a base, close to the Cambodian border, named Khe Sanh. In the late 1960s, Khe Sanh had become a slaughterhouse for the US Marine Corps. It was a large, flat area surrounded by heavily wooded hills. The marines were on the flat area, and the North Vietnamese were in the hills from which they poured mortar shells and rockets at the marines. In the middle of these attacks the flat area was cleared of vegetation and a short air strip was built. Clearing the vegetation made it even easier for the North Vietnamese to aim the mortars. The marines were visible. The enemy in the hills was not. More than a thousand marines would die. And for nothing.

A worse fighting position for the US could not have been imagined. Finding the enemy in the thick growth in the hills was nearly impossible, and the onslaught went on for weeks. At some point the marine command realized two things. First, that things were not going to get better, and second, that Khe Sanh was of absolutely no military value, or any other value. And had never been. Whoever made the decision to fight there should have been court-martialed and shot. But in the American forces he probably received a medal for bravery. In American military thinking hopelessness equaled bravery.

Also deserving to be shot was whoever decided in 1970 that the Americans — army and marines — plus a good number of ARVN troops should go back and reopen Khe Sanh to begin Operation Lam Son. I could imagine the North Vietnamese generals' disbelief when they were told by their intelligence people that the Americans were reestablishing in the exact place where so many of their people had been killed. There was a theory that to the enemy crazy equaled scary. It certainly worked for me. If the enemy could be convinced that the American leadership was crazy, they might be less inclined to continue fighting. Nixon's people toyed with the notion that if Ho Chi Minh thought Nixon had lost his reason, Ho would be more inclined to sue for peace. But Ho Chi Minh had decided on American insanity long before. Nixon was an afterthought.

Following the congressional rule against US soldiers

on the ground in Laos, ARVN troops were flown across the border, into the thickly covered Laotian mountains. The helicopters were piloted by Americans. The troops were South Vietnamese who were to be deposited on the tops of the mountains. That was about the only place pilots could safely land their helicopters. The enemy positioned itself on the sides of the mountains, where they could not be seen, and fired mortars upward to land on the summits. As soon as this was apparent, the South Vietnamese soldiers decided that they did not want to leave the American helicopters and refused orders to disembark. It is difficult to make soldiers leave a helicopter if they don't want to. Soldiers are all armed, which makes it even more difficult. Meanwhile mortars landed on the summits during the attempted landings. The entire operation, if it could be called that, descended into disobedience, revolt, and bloody chaos.

You must remember that the initial setting of the tone for this utter disaster, and for the war in general, was the fact that it was a civil war. The South Vietnamese people did not hate or even dislike the North. The northerners did not really hate the South. There was no religious hatred or revulsion between the two sides. In addition, the South Vietnamese, not hating the North, did not want to be in Laos and did not feel any passion worth dying for. And the North Vietnamese didn't want to be there, either. And the American pilots didn't want to be there and didn't hate anything worth getting shot out of the sky for. To make the helicopter pilots even less inclined to be energetic, the Russian heat-seeking missiles, compact items that could be shoulder-fired, were more plentiful. The rockets that sought out sources of heat in the air, like helicopter turbine exhausts, just to take an example, flew into the turbine exhausts and exploded. These weapons, maybe because of their Russian derivation, were not very accurate. But the threat was enough to make the American helicopter pilots wonder about getting home to their families. The pilots didn't really hate the North Vietnamese, or love the South. Their emotions were under constant review.

Within this whirl of desperately wrong military planning it was realized that if the troops on the ground were Vietnamese and the pilots in the air were American, a language disconnect had to be bridged. The American helicopters were armed with rockets, a pod of about thirty on either side of the ship. Ordinary land-based artillery was too far away from the invasion, and American artillery troops were not permitted to set up batteries on the Cambodian or Laotian side of the borders. Rockets from helicopters, or aerial rocket artillery, ARA, were inaccurate and hardly as plentiful as ground-based. In addition, since the pilots could not see where the enemy was hiding in the forests, they could fire their rockets only sort of generally, more or less, toward where they thought the enemy might be, and hope to hit something. And even if an ARVN unit called for a target to be hit, the rocket-firing helicopter pilots had another drawback. Where exactly was the target? Land-based artillery can be very accurate because the battery knows exactly where their guns are positioned, and they stay there. It can plot things like azimuth and elevation and drop a shell pretty accurately on an enemy unit. But helicopters are moving around and can only approximate their firing position. Needless to say, the aiming of rockets from helicopters is imprecise to the point of mere guesswork. The official military term for this is *non-discriminatory*, a term that sounds a little better than *all over the place*.

I had by that time a group of seven or eight ARVN interpreters, whose command of English was about the same as my command of Vietnamese. They were sort of assigned to me, and I was sort of their commander. But the relationship between us was a type of very worried collegiality. Like many squads with a knowledge of what was really going on we looked out for each other and talked over the situation frankly. We were even more worried when we were told to go north to assist in communication between the American pilots and ARVN troops in operations leading up to Lam Son. I had read of the plight of Napoleon's soldiers when he abandoned his foray in Russia, and my interpreters knew of the French defeat at Dien Bien Phu.

We were quartered with units of the 1st Air Cavalry and the 9th ARVN, forty or fifty miles more or less north of Saigon. Some of my interpreters had their families close by. The most senior of my interpreters was Sergeant Xuan, who was closest to me in age and temperament. He had children, and he was a worrier. He explained that although he would go north with me to see what the situation was like, the others had pretty much decided that . . . well, they had decided nothing, and I could decide for myself about their reliability. He was a friend I guess, whatever friendship means in really threatening situations. Sergeant Xuan and I talked everything over.

The prospect of deserting the South Vietnamese forces occurred to him, but there were obvious problems. First, desertion was punishable by a short hearing and then being shot. There was no open court-martial or due process. Second, Sergeant Xuan had spent several years in the ARVN; he had a family. He made little money, but it was still something. Third, no one knew what the outcome of the war would be — stalemate, reunification, defeat, or victory for the North. There would doubtless be a period of judgment and punishment. And lastly, the Americans might leave. The Americans had a track record of leaving their allies to deal with the messes they left behind. This is not widely reported, but it's true. Sergeant Xuan could not believe that the Americans would abandon the entire nation of South Vietnam, and frankly neither could I, or anyone I knew. But the possibility of an American abandonment, after all the expense and death, seemed to skirt the horizon like a line of tornadoes, a slowly approaching hell. Sadly, I thought that the US would stay in South Vietnam in one form or another if only to save face, if only because it would preserve their honor before the rest of the world, if only because they had never lost a war before. Xuan believed that and so did I. Amazing what you can believe when you are not thinking too clearly.

My orders, never written out but generally voiced by three different superior officers with inexact parameters, were that my interpreters and I would fly from where we were in the south up to a base near Khe Sanh, a firebase near the demilitarized zone. And there we would be assigned jobs listening to radio sends from the ARVN on the ground calling for more rockets or, as I could imagine, desperate calls for evacuation of the wounded. If the radio signals weren't clear enough, we would have to move as close to the Laotian border as needed. How close? Sergeant Xuan said he wasn't sure. I wasn't sure, either.

Coupled with my distrust of any army planning, my conviction that the South Vietnamese army would not do anything it was told was another factor that made me the wrong person to rely on. I was, as the term had it, short. I had less than a month left in my strange year in the war zone. Being able to have survived this far without getting killed as a result of all my dilatory cleverness made me even more fearful that, like a very mean-spirited joke, my story would end with me being blown apart within weeks of my ignoble goal. I couldn't sleep even though I knew that my apprehensions of Operation Lam Son were worse than the reality. I decided that I would obey the order and make additional plans en route.

We — six translators, Sergeant Xuan, and I — started north in a Chinook whose outer skin I distinctly remember was dented and scratched and filthy with dust and streaks of oil. Chinooks are twin-rotor transport helicopters, big clumsy things that could carry nearly a full platoon of soldiers and their gear. We shared the trip north with some utterly lost Vietnamese women and children. The military nature of this trip was not strengthened by weeping native women and bawling children. I never knew who they were exactly or why they were with us. Sergeant Xuan had fallen into silence. The trip was also very cold. On ground level the land is heavily humid and hot, but above about three thousand feet, the temperature drops. I was freezing. Odd what you remember.

We had to land at a base about halfway up South Vietnam in high country and wait for another aircraft. We waited several hours before the next leg of our journey, during which I noticed that my translators were walking off in all directions.

Sergeant Xuan came and told me how things were. The six ARVN translators were not going any farther north. They had taken their own counsel and deserted. Well, not exactly deserted since we really didn't know what our orders were. Nothing was written, and I could only generally explain our mission, if mission it was. In fact, Sergeant Xuan lowered his eyes and confessed that he wasn't going any farther, either. And to further add to my mood of compound foreboding, he advised me as my friend that he would warn me also to go no farther.

We had, by that time, come to know each other pretty well. He knew I was probably the worst soldier in the American army, and certainly the worst officer since Captain Yossarian, and that in his opinion whatever luck had kept me alive so far might be about to run out. The Vietnamese, like many Asians, have definite ideas about the role of luck in life. They believe that good luck is balanced by bad luck, and thus good luck is one of the worst things that can happen to you. I hadn't told him that I had less than a month left before I could go home honorably, but I was filled with dread, unequaled before or since. Most of my plans in the army had either failed or come to naught, so why should this be any different?

17

You will conclude, and I will agree with you, that I was
not a good soldier. My nonacceptance of any shame for
my stalwart avoidance of responsibility was solidified by
this time. General MacArthur gave a farewell speech to a
West Point class in which he stressed three themes. He
was a self-aggrandizing bloviator, but he used three words
to serve as touchstones for the American soldier, and
certainly the American officer. He counseled "Duty,
Honor, Country." If you fulfill these you have nothing to
be ashamed of. Ah, but saying these things is easy. The
argument then progresses to finer points of definition.
The words were abstractions. They belonged in songs
and prayers, not solid directions for what to do next. Had
I fulfilled these abstractions, or even two out of three?
Had I, for instance done my duty? And if I had, then how
much more was required as I flew north, toward a battle
ill defined and patently ill advised, and, while we're at
it, frankly unnecessary. MacArthur, in many examples,
showed that he had only marginal respect for the lives of
his men. Their duty was to follow orders, to do and die, to
advance and stop bullets coming at them. I could ask,
when considering my own obligations of duty, what
exactly were MacArthur's obligations, or any general officer's, to make sure that plans had some guarantee of

success. Was it anyone's duty at the top to balance costs against gain? On the other hand, how was a general expected to get anything done, how to effect a victory, if he couldn't depend on people to do what they were goddamn told?

If, as is now the case, the armed services had been filled with people, men and women, who volunteered for the dangers of military operations, then these people presumably would have known what the risks were inherent in their decision. If they didn't know, they should have been clearly told. But in an armed effort prompted by confused and abstract political aims, most of the soldiers in Vietnam were draftees, drafted under compulsion of imprisonment and other punishments. So what did duty actually mean? MacArthur would have countered that soldiers should shut up and obey. If they died or were grievously wounded, blinded or maimed, or driven crazy in their subsequent existence, had their family life ruined, came apart in their careers, became suicidal or murderous, and any combination of the foregoing, well, then that's the chance you take, not only in war but also in life. At least you and your family weren't speaking Japanese.

To further confuse the minds of the officer class, MacArthur added the word *honor*. I did not know then, and I do not know now, and I have never met anyone before or since the war, or any war, who can clearly tell me what the word means. It is situational. Performing a task that has serious costs, in pain or other deprivation, a task that you would rather not do, involves at least the idea of honor. Fulfilling an obligation, keeping a promise, being present at an expectation, all these are somehow and to some degree exercising honor. Checks are honored at the bank. Green stamps are honored for gifts. Insurance policies are honored when claims are made. Obligations to pay for elderly parents, sick children, business contract stipulations, and so on are all honored. But what about the honoring of an expectation to tell the truth if you know it? What about the honor to look out for the men, who are largely powerless, who were assigned to your command? I could go on, but you get the idea.

I also was bothered and ashamed at another characteristic of the American commanders, which was a disinclination to think. This may well be an American trait, a type of fat, dumb, and happy stumbling forward, counting on the wealth and size of the country to make everything come out okay. Officers I met and talked with, most of whom outranked me, met any doubt about the war with a practiced ignorance and a helpful stupidity, forging forward even if they were inwardly convinced of the wrongheadedness of what they were doing. And this wrongheadedness was present from the clumsy daily task and mission all the way to the enormity of the undefined mess of the Vietnam War, a war that after years of stasis and costs and blood had produced a worse situation than existed before it started.

Which left MacArthur's third abstraction — country. Most people think they know what this means, easily excluding all the variables that define the word. In the case of the American politicians who sent us to Vietnam, little consideration was given to the idea that Vietnam should have been defined by the Vietnamese themselves.

In later years it turned out that the Vietnamese didn't give a damn about the ravings and disastrous thinking of Marx or Mao or anyone. They wanted to be Vietnamese. Years of domination by the rapacious French and the disemboweling Japanese had made them love their land far more than the American glory hunters and jackass advisers loved theirs.

So I had lost my team of interpreters, and I was alone. I would not be able to decipher radio messages coming from ARVN units trapped on the top of Laotian mountains, screaming for medical evacuation, or more likely total evacuation as the North Vietnamese mortared them from the sides of the mountains. Journalists got hold of photos of the ARVN troops refusing to get off the helicopters, or hanging on to the struts, hanging on for what turned out to be comparatively dear life. Reports followed of US helicopter pilots refusing direct orders to fly the ARVN troops into Laos. Whatever value may have been present in obeying orders, whatever rewards there might have been for discipline or heroism, had disappeared. No one spoke of it. No one I ever met spoke of medals or promotions. No one. Well, maybe that general who had put himself in for a Silver Star for an act of heroism and bravery that turned out to be fictional, but he never spoke about it, either.

So by myself, with my minimal identification and my dictionary of Vietnamese military terms, my rifle, and my totally useless automatic .45, I got in the next helicopter and flew north.

18

There were effectively no front lines or rear areas in the Vietnam War. There were firebases with five or six guns, bunkers to house the troops, an open space for helicopters to land, a dug-out area to store the ammunition, and some sort of mess facility. Some firebases had been in place for years. An inevitable slovenliness set in. Huge rubber bladders of fuel leaked diesel and gasoline that mixed with the kitchen residue and other fluids. Uncontrollable fires were not uncommon, very frightening especially when they spread to the ammunition storage areas. Then frantic efforts had to be made to move artillery rounds to someplace, anyplace, safe. The firebases were of no particular design since the assumption was that they would not be needed for a long time and would be transferred to the ARVN troops as soon as they adequately trained in artillery aiming and ranging. A chain-link fence was erected around the firebase. Observation and radio towers were here and there. Each firebase had a commander who took the assignment for about six months. Some were strict about hygiene and security. Some weren't. Some firebases had grown with the amount of fighting around them, and some had shrunk to only two or three guns in the middle of a larger fenced area. But nearly all of them had something that was labeled an officers' club, or at least a hut with a sign in front.

The firebase where I finally landed during Operation Lam Son was called Firebase Matthew, or at least I think that was the name. I may have imagined it since Matthew was my baby son's name. I came with the unwelcome news that my interpreters had deserted and that all by myself I really could not understand numbers and directions screamed in terror by the ARVNs stuck on mountaintops in Laos. It was a larger-than-average firebase, and the officers' club was a little bit less disgusting than others I had seen. I went there first to try to get a sense of what was going on. I didn't know where I was supposed to report or to whom. I was told of the situation, of the desperately frightened and demoralized ARVN troops, of their equally frightened commanders, of our pilots who were increasingly disobedient. I was told that the situation in Laos was deteriorating daily, and other disasters were unfolding. The border area had never been properly mapped so we only had a rough idea of where the mountains and streams were. The land itself is very thick forest, and it is fair to say, although I never flew over it myself, that one mountain looked pretty much like another. In the army terminology troops were to be "inserted," and then they "conducted operations," and then they were "extracted." These anodyne descriptors sound good at a distance, but they are horrible close up. News of the second Khe Sanh ongoing disaster was well known and regarded as a predictor of defeat in Operation Lam Son. So then what would become of Firebase Matthew?

Armed with this frightening initial evaluation firmly in mind, I wandered around Firebase Matthew, from the officers' club to the headquarters, searching for someone of high rank or authority to report to. I may have made a less-than-ardent effort to report to the command, but confusion helped me along. After two days of odd dislocation, during which I found digs in a bunker with some ARVN soldiers and ate only canned scrambled eggs and ham, I had reached such a level of personal filth and fear that I needed direction. I went to the headquarters bunker and announced myself. The colonel in charge had decided to cover his confusion and helplessness with bombast and threats. Who was I, he wanted to know. What the hell was he supposed to do with me? Where were my translators? How had I allowed them to run off? What kind of shithead officer was I? He continued in this critical vein, very cross and confused. I knew enough about how to deal with the army by then to simply wait out the abuse and say as little as possible. He actually made me a little more confident, in a very strange way, when I realized that it wasn't just me who was unsure and disoriented. It was everyone.

Operation Lam Son at that time was only one of several Lam Sons and sons of Lam Son. The painful fact slowly became apparent that you couldn't stop a supply channel like the Ho Chi Minh Trail, wandering hundreds of miles through mountains and jungles, bringing food and medicine and ammunition to an army determined to stay and fight, especially if their main weapon was time. We bombed endlessly, we dropped poison and napalm on the forests, we bombed the places we had already bombed, and it did no good. I wondered why I could figure this out, but the generals and the political leaders could not. I came to feel a bit sorry for General Abrams, now handed an impossible assignment and who would end his otherwise long, proud career shepherding a bloody mess toward the escape hatch, but actually not much. Also, by this time the journalists who covered the war were convinced that there was no chance of victory. Many of them realized that however it ended it would be, at least for American soldiers and the American people, nothing short of a shame to be forgotten. It would be hard to forget. Few journalists predicted that it would take another five years to the American withdrawal. The closest to wisdom I heard from a journalist was that a Korea-like standoff was the best the US could hope for. I believed that for a while, along with a group of things I also believed that turned out wrong.

So I had an amusing, if you are amused by fear and loathing, situation. I was on this noisy, godforsaken place, in the middle of a war, in the midst of disgusted American soldiers and their hopeless allies, under commanders trying to effectuate a battle plan with tactics designed and compromised by the disputatious and ignorant American politicians back in Washington. The fighting went on, and the casualties mounted. Some American helicopters were shot down, a very hard way to end your military career. Helicopter pilots were warrant officers, a rank that is reserved for persons who have special skills. They are not as respected as regular officers, and in a way, they know it. They do what they do because they love to fly, not necessarily to fight and kill. They are workmen doing a valuable job, and they expect to be intelligently used

— certainly not thrown into a battle as a desperate measure. During Operation Lam Son many American pilots, probably more than will ever be admitted, refused orders to fly across the Laotian border. The orders were pretty much suicidal. I repeat that a helicopter in the sky can be seen and heard. A North Vietnamese on the ground, in the thick forest, carrying a weapon or a Russian surface-to-air missile, is invisible. The missions were definitely suicidal. And suicide has to have a better reason than simply that someone orders you to do it.

19

So, what did I do?

I was probably more aware than most troops of the larger combat situation at the time, with all the faults and fraudulent explanations Washington had made. I could see the military situation then more clearly than what many on the ground at Khe Sanh and the various firebases could see. I could see more than the American infantry troops, who were given only the briefest account of historical relevance to what they were asked to do and the risks they were made to take. I could see what the real relationship was between the American army and the South Vietnamese army. I could see all this clearly, even if on the surface I looked like a clever shirker and as if I were willing to let others take the risks. I could see that the troops, both the South Vietnamese and the Americans, were being killed for the basest of political reasons.

So, what did I do?

I had to do something, in the midst of all this confusion, using my questionable ability to interpret radio messages between the South Vietnamese on the ground and the American pilots in the air. There were some ARVN troops who had some English and could relay panic calls for artillery and bombing runs and medevac help. But someone had to determine the truth in their reports. Did they know what they were talking about, what they were asking for? How and to what extent could the Americans do anything? I tried to explain to the colonel who had gone from screaming insults at me to now threatening me with a court-martial. I said that a court-martial would be fine with me. I gave my opinion that the planning for this operation and all the attendant operations was wrongly composed, unrealistic, and ignorant of the endless dangers inherent. I used shorter Anglo-Saxon words, but the point was the same. I said that we were being used for purposes that were largely theatrical. I said that we were being thrown away, along with our allies, as the regrettably expendable assets because the American politicians feared being blamed for a military loss and would do anything to cover their reputations. A court-martial, while not welcome, was no threat. In the midst of all the noise and confusion a court-martial had no weight at all.

So, what did I do?

No court-martial was ever convened or even mentioned again. The colonel screamed some more and then turned to screaming at someone else. I left him not knowing if he would actually do anything. I didn't care. I worked for a few days with an ARVN air support unit, trying to orient their maps, since this area of Laos was irregularly mapped many years ago by French troops. All this time I watched the days elapse, about three weeks until I had less than a week still required in country. An American soldier was only made to stay in Vietnam one year. At the end of the year you got orders for DEROS, the date en route overseas, the date to escape the year that seemed like ten.

Some troops actually signed up for a second year, and even a third if they considered their duty more interesting than a return to some unpleasant American life. I didn't consider that an option, because not only was my obligation in Vietnam coming to an end, but my obligation to the army was over as well. Returning to the States meant returning to civilian life, a job if there was one, and a completely new set of circumstances.

In the three weeks the ARVN air operations group, in which I was never sure who had the job of commander, suffered more men lost and helicopters shot down. Their helicopters had suspicious mechanical complaints. The Vietnamese pilots and the repair troops were sloppy, and they didn't trust machinery like Americans did. The repair facilities were farther back inside Vietnam. In the whole operation more than a hundred helicopters were lost, shot down, or rendered unflyable. I noticed that a lot of the ARVN helicopters were tagged as not reparable and had to be flown or airlifted back to a safer place to be fixed. This was preferable to flying into Laos. Anything was preferable to flying into Laos.

I waited, putting all my now considerable dilatory skills into the appearance of activity, and counting the days. I joined some missions at night, some in the early morning, when the dark or the low light made the helicopters less visible. Helicopters ran into each other, or tried to land near unseen trees or wires. I went to a few situation briefings, with the mad idea that I would be able to help the Vietnamese understand what the Americans were talking about. It was an endless stream of disaster, loss, retreat, missed communications, unsolvable disputes, raw emotions, and old hatreds. Picking up ARVN troops from the tops of mountains while being shot at was terrifying. A Huey could only get off the ground with nine or ten soldiers, and when more than that wanted to get on, and were ready to fight for the right, not only did the helicopter itself fail to go up, but the pilot's control disappeared as well. At the morning briefings one general objected to allowing Vietnamese officers to attend, because he suspected they might be passing plans and other information to the North. This meant intentionally keeping our supposed allies in the dark. I thought this was wrong, and I said so, although I only partially understood myself. This was a period of time when I didn't care what I said. I sensed that my attempts to translate either had no effect or actually made things worse. The briefings were held in a dark bunker, half underground, and each morning's report was begun with a chaplain offering an unspecific Catholic prayer, which, for the Buddhist Vietnamese, was untranslatable.

My plans were to run the clock out and leave. Other Americans would still be here. Others would continue to mount operations, forays into Laos, rescue flights, and reinforcement missions. Vietnamese and Americans were killed or wounded every day, every day that I counted down to my escape. I will admit that somewhere in a very small part of my conscience I wondered if, fundamentally, in the most basic part of my humanity, the right thing would be to stay and see Operation Lam Son through, for as long as it took. Seeing bodies coming back from Laos, with dead ARVNs strapped to the floor of

Hueys, with blood covering the floor of the ship, and then the body taken out on a stretcher, and the blood hosed away, was enough to enrage some part of me. But was it enough? There was a chance that rage would replace self-preservation, and the only way to counter this was to not look. If the greater part of the American people could look away, why couldn't I?

What solidified my conviction was hearing a speech by Nixon, I am sure written by someone of his political staff, also not present in Vietnam, to the effect that "the Vietnamese people have taken up the burden of their own freedom," or something like that — a completely uncaring lie concocted to beguile the voters into thinking that some sort of plan was working. And I can remember that I felt even more strongly, stronger than I had ever felt before, that I was on my own. I felt that duty and honor and country were all secondary to taking care of my own skin.

So, what did I do? Let me answer with a question.

20

What would you do?

First the draft. Would you obey a notice from the United States government to stop your life at home, forestall your plans, leave your family and friends, leave the many comforts and privileges of American life, leave your ideas about personal accomplishment and reward, leave your desires for wealth and property? Would you do all this because you trusted people in power? Would you even question what they were telling you to do? Would you obey or object or refuse when you sensed that you were chosen by a draft system and a draft board that exempted your contemporaries still in college, or others they were trying to protect?

Could they make you into a soldier? Would you accept forced military training? Would you present yourself to obey orders and training making you into a trained killer? A killer of people you didn't know and had no quarrel with? In a country you had never heard of? To eradicate an economic system like communism, something you had only the faintest knowledge of and didn't care about? Would you be able to tolerate being yelled at by drill sergeants and others, made to perform idiotic and archaic military drills? Could you stand being, in effect, ostracized by an American culture that was dead set against the war and everything you were doing? The cultural message came through loud and clear in music, in daily journalism, in political posturing, in movies and television. Could you stand the loneliness of the training bases hundreds of miles from home with only the companionship of other men equally lonely and miserable?

What would you decide if you were told to do an irretrievable act, something violent and deadly? What if you had to shoot someone? A supposed enemy? What would you do if the logic of enemies came forward? The logic of enemies, my own term, is that if you don't shoot the enemy, he will shoot you. This argument is exactly mirrored on the other side. It exists with its own internal unanswerable mechanics. You are not attacking. You are defending. You have the right to defend. You and the enemy are both defending.

Things worth considering: The decision to pull the trigger and kill an enemy soldier, to hear the gun, to see him grimace and fall, and to know that you had killed someone would make a line across your life. You would be a different person. You would instantly, and from that time forward, be capable of all manner of things you did not think you were capable of. You were now part of that uneasy fraternity of people who had killed another person.

But who would you be defending? Obviously, you would be defending, or helping to defend, your fellow soldiers. But you would be defending more than that. You would be defending the commanders of your unit who had gotten you into the firefight, or at least failed to get you out of it. You would be defending the command structure over them. You would be defending everyone, in my case up to General Abrams and Ellsworth Bunker, the vicious old US ambassador to Vietnam, back in Saigon safely at the embassy, conferring with the president of Vietnam, Nguyen Van Thieu, whom I was also defending, and so on up a list of people in the American government including Richard Nixon.

Could you push back against a future of being internally haunted by the question *Why am I doing this?* Could you summon the bravery — or the internal resistance — to simply refuse to be part of the whole idiotic theater of the war? Could you agree that it really was the universal soldier who really was to blame, as the song said? And that unless you did something *you* were the universal soldier?

Or would you be like me? Planning a secret internal defense against all the doubt and discomfort of protest and wanting simply to not stand out and not be seen as different. It is not the soldier's job to think, but they do it anyway.

In Vietnam, at some point a soldier inevitably sensed that the army itself was damaged beyond repair, and from then on he was no longer a soldier. He was simply a person in a horrid situation that had to be suffered until a solution or an escape came along. The draftees in Vietnam, and even some of the regular career officers and non-coms, may have been guilty, probably the wrong word, of retreating, secretly, selfishly. Retreat is after all a tactic.

And then there is the question of who was responsible, who was in charge. Was anyone? Commanders, from General Abrams on down, may also have been guilty of abandoning the mission, of turning their backs on the possibility of victory. They could have said, look, we can't win. But they never said that. They could argue that they were doing their duty. But they had a duty not to use the lives of their soldiers in pursuit of defeat. What they did not do was loudly make the point that the war should be abandoned. In this decision there was still a small element of their own self-preservation. I would also argue that they were paralyzed by the realization that, with all these people, all this money, and all these weapons, there would be no success, no stalemate, nothing that even had the outward appearance of a worthwhile conclusion. There would be only embarrassment, loss, bitter dissolution, and more endless waste. If the fates showed any mercy the disaster would happen quickly and they, the US, the country, could get on to the next thing. It would require a huge amount of energetic pretense. But if the Wehrmacht could do it, if the defeated Japanese could do it, if the countless defeated armies in human history could do it, then we could do it. Anyway, we had no choice.

21

So, what I did was I left Firebase Matthew and the ongoing violence of Operation Lam Son. I flew back south to Phuoc Vinh, and from there to Bien Hoa. I had my papers showing that I had been in Vietnam a year and had fulfilled my obligation. Not only was my time in country done, but as I said, my time in the army was nearly over. With DEROS orders in hand I made my way to the 90th Replacement Depot near Tan Son Nhat, Saigon's airport. I spent three lonely nights there, watching the planes take off for the States and writing home that I would be there soon. The letters would not get home before me, but I didn't care. I was added to a roster of men scheduled for return, some of whom were happy, but not as happy as they thought they might be. The prevailing mood was one of relief, of having survived where others didn't. The three days moved slowly. I also noticed that there was anticipation for what return would mean. What we had all looked forward to for the year in the war was now real, with everything that went with it — unemployment, survival, disappointment, and the discovery of what had happened to family, wives, and children in our absence. Some people would be happy to see us, but maybe not as many as we thought. It was no secret — this was not going to be a glorious return. We were not returning heroes. We were returning to a defeated country regardless of how the definition of defeat was now reconstructed. There would be no parades, no welcomes, no special benefits. With some luck we could blend into the background of American life and not talk about Vietnam unless someone asked, or even then.

Each soldier waiting to return home carried his entire folder of orders, assignments, units, disciplinary actions and punishments, health, and in some cases wounds and treatments. All on paper. There were several men on my plane who were bandaged, had limbs bound up, and some were on crutches. Some were weak and had to have assistance getting on the bus to the airport. Even after all this time and experience there was evidence of racial separation, which I thought was amazing and sad.

I was the only officer on the plane so I was detailed to carry the manifest of names and units. The plane was a private carrier, Air America or Flying Tiger or something. Again, a private company making money off the war. No alcohol was permitted. Eighteen hours of sullen, rather miserable flying without even the slight relief that booze would have provided, again proving the army's ability and inclination to make anything that was already miserable and boring even more so.

22

We landed at Travis Air Force Base near San Francisco at a little before midnight. Most of the troops on the plane took off for the city and a good time. Some stood in wonder that they were actually back. Some stood in line for telephones to call home. I turned in my rosters and other paperwork and then wondered what I would do. My wife was in Denver with our baby son at her parents' house. So no one was there to meet me.

There was a tradition in the army that when you returned from the war zone you qualified for a supposedly quintessential American meal — steak, fries, and for dessert strawberry shortcake with whipped cream. I had heard about this and wanted to see if it was true. I made my way to the air force mess hall, open, as many air force mess halls are, around the clock. It was a large place with several hundred tables. It was empty except for me. Almost as empty as I felt. I took a chair and waited.

A cook stuck his head out of the kitchen.

"You want your meal?"

"Yes."

He disappeared and after about twenty minutes reappeared. He set the steak platter and the dessert bowl on the mess line counter.

"Get yourself a tray," he said and disappeared again.

I cannot say that I got nothing for my military time. I returned a serious person, much more so than I was before. And I am now receiving Social Security with a few additional dollars for being a veteran. I got some medals, a Bronze Star and an Air Medal. The Bronze Star either means that I did something of which I am not aware, or means that the Bronze Star means nothing.

It is also the case that I gained, without actually getting shot, some knowledge of what war is like. This allows me to read bloody sections of history and strife not as abstractions but as scenes I can clearly picture. I never sought this knowledge, but now that I have it, I am stuck with it. In addition, I can more accurately judge, and in most cases dismiss, the claims made by the shallow and rotten politicians who seek fame and renown on the backs of credulous soldiers. This knowledge does not make anyone happy, but neither does most other wisdom. Maybe it just adds to the accuracy of a person's self-direction and judgment as life situations present themselves. I think I trust much less, and in some cases not at all. I accept almost nothing on face. I am not grumpy or rude, but I can almost immediately detect a lie or a half-truth or an opportunistic claim or an abstraction paraded as something real. And I often detect a lie, sadly, even when there isn't any. This is not an advantage.

On a more practical level it means that I can meet the cowards of the right and the fools of the left with a simple stare and a few words of cold dismissal. Of course, as you can tell, I enjoy doing this, and seize every opportunity.

I have some distant brotherly feelings for my fellow

Vietnam War veterans, but I have avoided get-togethers or veteran organizations, and this book is a rare storytelling session for me.

I have some young friends who are veterans of the Iraq and Afghanistan wars. Some are horribly wounded. It occurs to me that Vietnam draftees had one advantage that today's voluntary enlistees do not have. Draftees during Vietnam knew that the situation was going to be miserable and ultimately awful, whereas the volunteer army today has to find all that out.

I learned, and I think most veterans learn, that making people or nations do something by bombing or sending in armed troops usually fails. People are disobedient in direct proportion to the armed attempts to make them obedient. The more troops the less chance of lasting success. The armed forces have two jobs — to kill people and to blow things up. The usually young men and women who compose them are often repulsed by orders to do either of those things. Armies do not — WHAM — win hearts and minds. If there is any discipline at the start of wars it dissipates as the soldiers themselves become aware of the pointlessness of what they are being told to do.

I came back in 1971 and immediately needed a job. The war was dying, and the US economy declined along with it. I got a job teaching school, which I did for about ten years. I think I was a good teacher, in part because I compared my American students with the children who grew up in Vietnam during the war. I don't know exactly what effect this comparison had on my attitude toward my students, but I think I was more realistic and maybe more demanding than I would have been otherwise. Without the slightest pause I rejected the theoretic claptrap that was offered by the education schools. I was not a disciplinarian, but I could see that the concocted abstractions of psychologists and sociologists when applied to public school students were little more than handy excuses for failure. This makes me sound to the right politically, but I am not. I simply distrust abstractions. Being successful, or even secure, in the United States — the sad, silly United States — requires a hard-eyed evaluation applied daily, to everything.

A war can provide a realistic attitude and a knowledge of what human existence actually is, of what can be expected, and how much you can trust your fellow citizens and your nation. This is hard to teach. I wanted to do it while teaching, but I kept these thoughts and statements at a minimum. It was not my job or wish to create cynics before it becomes absolutely necessary. I got some understanding from my high school students. Some accepted and adopted my gloomy attitude, but others thought I was simply an adult and therefore not to be credited.

After I had been teaching for a few years a student, not knowing what he was asking, asked me if I had killed anyone. I was a little shocked that anyone cared. But if you are going to discuss the war, or any war, with the idea of warning another generation about the slide into conflict, you should tell the whole story.

I didn't shoot anyone that I knew of. But it was true that I shot at them, or somebody. Some people I couldn't see. In several instances, in contacts with the ARVN and in the rubber plantation with the 11th Armored Cavalry

Regiment, and other firefights where confusion and fear were in control, I fired with everyone else. I had no idea where the bullets went, and perhaps they did hit another human being. I don't know, and it's just a little comforting that I don't know. Of course, I knew what I was doing. I knew what bullets did, and I knew that just being in a trap of circumstance wasn't enough of a justification.

We are now about two full generations from the ignoble closing of the fighting between the United States and Vietnam. Amazing changes have occurred. You can now buy garments and products of decent quality made in Vietnam. China, the former wellspring of Marxist and Maoist forces, is now as capitalist as can be. If there is another war it will be a world war. No one will escape. Scientific destruction will be unchallenged, and this country will call for soldiers, as usual, young men and women. The fifty-five thousand dead in the Vietnam War will seem like a pittance by the time it's over.

As time goes on and I get older, I am more haunted by my own history, with more questions today than yesterday. I can say that writing helps, and if you've read this far, you have my thanks. What the Vietnam War meant is still a mystery. What lessons can be learned are clouded by interpretations, even if some lessons should rightly be ignored. We may not know what the war meant, but we do know that it meant something. Still, the history is frightening. We can hear what Mao Tse-tung may have said when he was asked what the French Revolution meant.

He said, "It's too early to tell."

And if that doesn't scare the hell out of you, nothing will.